A Place on Water

Peter D. Nordgren

Copyright © 2025 Peter D. Nordgren
All rights reserved
Non-fiction: Nature/Essays

Design by Jamey Penney-Ritter,
Bemused Creative, Washburn, WI
www.bemusedposters.com

Edited by Dr. Deborah Davis Schlacks

Cover photo by by the author
Bayfield County Forest, Wisconsin

No part of this publication may be reproduced, distributed, or transmitted in any form or by any means, without prior written permission of the copyright holder, except in the case of brief quotations embodied in critical reviews and certain other noncommercial uses permitted by copyright law. For permission requests, write to the publisher at the address below.

North Branch
22140 Old Highway 13
Cornucopia, Wisconsin 54827
www.northbranch.info
northbranchbooks@gmail.com

Library of Congress Control Number: 2025900695
ISBN: 979-8-218-58814-4

For Deb
The best and bravest partner
for any adventure of life

For Eric & Todd
May they never be far
from the woods and water

Contents

In the Beginning		1
Building	Common Blackberry	5
Exploring	Eastern Beaked Hazel	8
Remembering	Eastern Teaberry	12
Observing	Pileated Woodpecker	15
Watching	Northern Barred Owl	18
Shining	Black-eyed Susan	21
Cruising	Double Striped Bluet Damselfly	24
Snowing	Winterberry	27
Leaping	Northern Leopard Frog	30
Glowing	Ghost Pipes	34
Seeking	Common Redpoll	37
Rising	Canada Mayflower	40
Floating	Yellow Pond-Lily	43
Clinging	Little Brown Bat	47
Towering	Eastern White Pine	54
Investigating	Black-capped Chickadee	51
Conversing	American Crow	57
Delighting	Juneberry	61
Hopping	American Toad	64
Adopting	Red-winged Blackbird	67
Branching	Staghorn Sumac	72
Probing	North American Deer Mouse	75
Growing	Aspen	78
Surviving	Western Painted Turtle	82
Falling	Northern Red Oak	87

CONTENTS

Multiplying	Common Merganser	90
Roaming	Eastern Timber Wolf	93
Gliding	Eastern Garter Snake	96
Communing	Eastern Chipmunk	99
Flocking	Evening Grosbeak	102
Penetrating	Black Carpenter Ant	104
Blazing	Northern Blue Flag	107
Amusing	Raccoon	110
Dominating	Bracken Fern	113
Calling	Coyote	116
Wading	Great Blue Heron	119
Marching	Forest Tent Caterpillar	122
Consuming	American Black Bear	125
Darting	Ruby-throated Hummingbird	128
Perplexing	Mystery Bush	131
Diving	Great Northern Loon	134
Sliding	North American River Otter	137
Annoying	Eastern Black-legged Tick	140
Glowing	Tamarack	144
Pursuing	Fisher	147
Persisting	Northern Paper Wasp	151
Striking	Largemouth Bass	154
Wandering	White-tailed Deer	159
Uplifting	Paper Birch	162
Sheltering	Eastern Phoebe	165
In the End		169

IN THE BEGINNING

It begins with a small hand-painted wooden sign nailed to a skinny popple tree. The tree, wet from rain, stands along a dead-end road in the uplands twenty miles south of Lake Superior. The road winds back on the south edge of a high, maple-covered ridge. I know there's a large lake somewhere over the hill to the north. Across the road is the tree with the sign. Chipped green paint, hand-drawn letters, "For Sale By Owner." Beyond, a glint of water.

I'm driving this road in search of the place to raise my family. I have a new job nearby, so Deb and I are relocating several hundred miles northwest across the Wisconsin forests. Our firstborn, Eric, is nearly three; our second child, Todd, will be here in a few months. Like most of the people we know, we've always thought of a home on a lake for ourselves and our children. We don't have much in our bank account, and waterfront land is always the highest priced. We need a special deal to fulfill our hopes.

I stop the car and walk down through the damp hazel brush toward the shore. Behind the popples there's a small opening, then tall, arching oaks and maples nearer the water. It's spring, and there's not much green in the woods, but a few pines and balsams are scattered here. I push through the brush to where the sky opens out. The lake is not quite round, not too big. I'll learn later it's ten acres. It's Northwoods picture-pretty, with tall red pines off to the southwest and a few bold white pines, the favorite tree of the North, on another glacial rise above the southern shoreline. Around the curve of the water, a few houses look out from the shore, each screened by a separating patch of woods. That's a good sign; we would have neighbors who respect the lake, who know enough not to run lawns down to the shore.

Everyone likes a sandy beach, but there isn't one here. The water's edge is attended by wetland plants, sedges and iris. A few lily pads have already sensed the warmth of the new season and popped to the surface. To my left, beyond leaning trunks of red oak and birch, I spot a bog, a tiny pocket of muskeg and alder brush, tucked back in a bay on the next property.

Yes, this place has promise. There's a dry slope where a house can rest on the rise above the water, in an opening dominated by thick blackberry canes. The house would face south and a bit west, good for some solar gain through lake-facing windows. The drive entry would be level, and there's electric power across the road.

Hiking back to the car, I write down the Green Bay area phone number from the sign. Later that day, a call to the owner confirms the land is still available. It seems there was a plan for a vacation cabin here, but a divorce took those dreams away. Now it might be the place of our dream, the place where our children can grow among the trees, by the water.

We pay earnest money, and on a windy day punctuated by fat raindrops, my friend Ray and I pound in stakes to mark what might be the corners of the house to come. But financing complications slow things down. For two years, in fact. We're young, and the people behind the big desks lack confidence in our income. Still, the dream stays in our life, and the owner is patient with us. Finally comes another rainy day in the fall, when a check is delivered to the owner's residence and exchanged for the deed. I leave our scruffy rented house, drive over a few miles to the lot, and pull the sign off the popple. It's ours.

What we now own is something shaped like a roughly cut chunk of pie. It's 215 feet on the road side, narrowing down to 120 feet on the lake, none of the four sides the same length. The record that goes to the Register of Deeds in the big gray courthouse tells us we are now taxpayers for 0.69 acres. We've had time to prepare, and our plans are in order. It will not be long before there will be backhoes, concrete trucks, and carpenters, and we'll see the walls rise up where we'll spend our days. We know, though, there's much more here: trees, plants, animals, fish, and frogs. So much is here, waiting to happen.

Our small parcel of the North already has many stories in its earth, its water, its sky. The Superior lobe of the Wisconsin glacier shaped it, dropping gravel and boulders as it melted away, washing and gullying the surface. When the water no longer scraped them away, small plants and bushes could gain a toehold. Hundreds of years later, there were trees. Native people walked among them, across this land, their Mother

Earth. It was their place for uncounted centuries, natural as the sun and moon. But nothing can stay the same forever, and change came unbidden, unexpected. The land would be ceded to others, first the Dakota to the Anishinaabe, then the Anishinaabe to the people from across the water. Trappers and traders came, then loggers, then farmers, and then someone who saw the value of this rise of ground simply as a place to live.

This thought, that satisfaction and pleasure could be found in a living space surrounded by these woods, by this lake, in this community of living things, is the story my family and I hope to create as we live here. We don't know this place yet, but we know we will. If we are observant and patient, we can come to understand something of it and to love it.

BUILDING

Common Blackberry
Rubus allegheniensis

It's spring again. Just a few patches of snow remain, and the woods are drying out. The house is not yet started. The stakes Ray and I put in are still there, but already weathered gray and leaning, obsolete. We needed them to show the appraiser where the house would stand, and the local government where the septic system would go. But the real footprint of the house we've now planned will be different. We're here today to put in the true corner markers, the ones that will guide the basement digging and foundation pouring.

The stakes stick out of the patch of native berries. This opening and the presence of the popple mean that not long ago, this part of the lot was not woods. Neighbors have told us this was part of a farm. The farmhouse and barn sites were a few lots west, up the rise a bit. As we push our way down through the brambles and into the narrow band of oak-maple woods along the shore, we cross a subtle change in the ground.

It's the track of an old farm road. If we trace it downhill toward the southeast corner of the lot, near the place where the shore meets the bog, we come across a few fist-sized stones. This small rock pile was left by the farmer, evidence of the back-straining work of turning glacial ground into a crop field or pasture. Most likely pasture. This is Wisconsin, and even here in the North dairying has been the favored way to coax a living out of the land. Cows once meandered across our lot, savoring the grasses and marching to the barn for milking hour.

The blackberries must have grown around the back of the barn and along the pasture edges. Wherever there is sun, this ambitious member of the rose family can get a toehold. While the sharp, grabby canes can be annoying, the farm people who lived here probably liked the blackberry, thinking of it as a nice bonus on a hardscrabble Northwoods farm. In a dish with sugar, in a bowl with cream, or baked in an aromatic pie, the king fruit of the woods can bring quiet satisfaction at the far edge of summer.

The blackberry fruits late because it blooms late. It will be mid-June before the white-petaled flowers are out, peeking from among the pert green leaves along the prickling stems. Late blooming means safety from frost, and on the other end of the calendar, a touch of the 30s doesn't really bother. When the blackberry blossoms appear, they tell us that spring has run its course.

We seem to have two kinds of blackberries here. In addition to the traditional waving canes, there is a creeping, viney style of plant that lies close to the ground, concealing its flowers and fruit. Some call these dewberries. You need a sharp eye to find them, cautiously lifting up the ground-hugging canes to pick the juicy reward.

But most of this berry patch will not blossom again. Next weekend I'll be here with a borrowed chainsaw, dropping the popples and limbing them up, moving the logs away. They'll thump down among the canes, crushing the leaves, releasing a strong, verdant smell. Then a man with a bulldozer will come, ramming up the stumps, shoving the sandy soil around, leveling up the house site for the backhoe, the concrete forms, the hulking ready-mix trucks. When the excavating and landscaping are finished, only a few of the low blackberry vines will be left growing by the new driveway. In the next few years, we'll enjoy their fruit on our cereal. Then, like all of their kind, they will lose vigor and stop bearing; new vines won't appear.

Our new neighbors down the road tell us they miss their local blackberry patch, though they like having us here. Price of progress…I guess.

EXPLORING

Eastern Beaked Hazel

Corylus cornuta
cornuta

I get up early and look out the big windows of our new home. I can see it all from here, but I slip on shoes and walk quietly out on the driveway to look more closely at the place we now own. We and the credit union, of course.

The driveway comes off the blacktop road near the high point, not far from the northwest corner. A young white pine grows here, starting to reach out over the road; the local municipality may have something to say about it in the future. We will keep it trimmed back and out of trouble. The rest of the tree cover here is small maples and popples. As I head downslope along the west side of the house, the timber gets bigger, and soon I pass the largest trees. Here are several huge maples and oaks that blanket this corner of the lot with their canopies, just back from the lakeshore. Their trunks, deeply gullied with age and the strain of growth, give this part of the property a flavor of mature forest. The people who farmed here must have cared about these trees; they were spared from the saw and the woodpile.

When I reach the lake, the shoreline is first bushes, then grasses. Turn and walk east along the curving boundary between land and water. One cannot truly walk the shore—there's no beach—but a few yards back, there's good going through ferns and some hazel brush. The hazel is the waist-high understory for much of the property, as it is in many forests in northern Wisconsin. This tenacious shrub of the birch family feeds the squirrels and chipmunks. They perform gymnastic feats while clambering up its skinny stalks to get at the green-husked nuts. We might like to try a few, but often these native hazelnuts are small and wormy. This doesn't bother the fuzzy rodents, who are always there first anyway.

As I walk east, I first cross the path that leads down through the maples, then pass the big oak reaching out from the shoreline into the lake's open light. Beyond is our larger of two white pines on the lot. This one is entering maturity, not yet one of the giants of the forest but on its way to being one.

Looking out across the water, I see a pair of mallards working the lily pad beds that bound the east and north sides of the lake. Water plants are their staple diet. They dip and nibble, feeding quietly at the edges. Above us all a brightening sky, a little sweep of cloud hinting at a chance of rain later.

Our metal property-corner rod stands a few feet out into the bog bushes, just back from the lakeshore. I turn northeast here and walk through the narrow grassy zone between bog and forest. Our boundary with our neighbors is somewhere within a few feet of this transition. The little bog is covered with knee-high bushes: sweet gale, leatherleaf, Labrador tea. A few tag-alders sprout up here and there; in time they may take over. Cattails line the edge where wetland becomes water. Out in the middle, the wettest part of the bog, a little tamarack has taken root, standing up out of a brushy clump of alder, its brand-new, light-green needles jumping out of the dark background.

Now I am back in the woods. Here, too, are mature red maples and red oaks, sixty or more feet in height, creating a cool, leafy space below. There is a little channel, a small gully of sorts, off to my right, on the neighbor's property. It doesn't look like much, and no water flows there. But when our lake was a hulking block of melting glacial ice, ten thousand years ago or so, this channel drained the meltwaters down to the nearby big lake. If you follow it across the road, it becomes a deep, water-cut ravine, right down to the shoreline.

The ice block was dirty, and the silt it dropped was enough to seal up the bottom of our lake so it holds water today, perched almost fifty feet above the level of the larger lake just a few hundred yards to the north. A little less silt and it would not have held water, becoming instead a low wet spot, or else a frost pocket, a dry bowl-shaped depression in moraine where cold air pools at night. More dirt, and it would have filled up with silt; it would be a swamp. But the amount was just right, and so we have a lake before our windows.

A few more steps, and I reach the road. Here, there is a patch of small popples, trees that, judging from their size, have sprung up in the past ten or fifteen years. They've filled in the former pasture, growing tightly together, just a few feet separating each slim trunk. For walking through the woods, a stretch of young popple matches an alder swamp for tough going, requiring the hiker to squeeze through tight spaces while receiving twigs and leaves in the face and down the neck. I'm grateful for the option of the paved route ahead. Walking back west, up the slope along the blacktop, a gray squirrel bounces across, mouth stuffed with something, possibly hazelnuts. I turn in at the driveway and go to search for my own breakfast.

Remembering

Eastern Teaberry
Gaultheria procumbens

I'm six years old. My mother is kneeling in the woods along the winding driveway to our family cabin on Hanscom Lake. "Peter, smell this." I sniff at the thick, shiny green leaf she folded in her fingers. It smells like a stick of gum. "It's wintergreen. They use this plant to flavor the gum. You can chew on it." I pluck one and munch away. The sweet, fresh flavor is immediate. I don't stop at one. "Here, try a berry." The dark red berry is mealy, with a less intense version of the pungent green essence.

My meeting with wintergreen at an early age, forty-some miles southwest of my current home, is one of my first memories of the forest. I learned to look for this ground-loving plant in the moist woods near lakes. True to its name, it emerges no worse for wear when the snowmelt drains away, ready for the season of slow growth and berry development.

I was warmed to find it growing near our shore, between the house and the lake, where the white pine keeps things a bit shady and not too dry. When the mounds of cold, white winter turn gray, with flecks of woods debris and crumbling crystals, the wintergreen begins to peek out, shining and smooth. Whenever I like, I can walk down and pick a leaf, fold it in half, and find again the strong scent I first found at Hanscom Lake. I chew the leaf. It has a trace of bitterness to it, but its essence speaks of cleanliness and shiny teeth. It reminds me of the healthy, deep green heart of the woods.

Wintergreen must be a beloved plant almost everywhere, since it has earned so many names. It seems it is called teaberry in the majority of places, and also goes by ground tea, grouseberry, deerberry, box berry, red pollum, and many others. In some places, it goes by drunkards, suggesting its ability to cover up alcohol on the breath, plucked from the roadside during an unsteady walk home. Like many plants that hug the ground, it carries the flag of the heath family, cousin to the similarly round-fruited blueberry and the equally pungent, though very differently scented, sweetfern.

Surrounding the wintergreen is another plant that shows green through the snowmelt, princess pine. My high school yearbook was named for this low-growing, ancient club moss. Though it looks fragile, it might be the most durable of all the living things we can see on our parcel of land. Its ancestors grew before there were any seed-bearing plants; its kind are millions of years older than the first wintergreen and the first white pine. Where I grew up, it was gathered for holiday decorations, despite the fact it's not a pine at all. Tacked to a Yule log, it does look pretty.

The princess pine produces spores, and the wintergreen has its berries, but both survive mostly by running rhizomes through the soil, sprouting up, when conditions are right, in wider circles. I imagine them stretching out below my feet, routing around stones and roots, sensing for the right conditions to seek the sunlight. So much of what makes a forest is unseen; not only the tree roots, not only the rhizomes, but the countless bacterial, fungal, and insect elements that live in the soil and exert their great influences on the parts we see above ground.

The small patch of wintergreen on our property allowed me to re-create my wintergreen introduction for Eric and Todd. Walking in the woods by the lake one day, feeling the warmth of spring sunshine, I knelt and plucked a pair of leaves. Folding them to crack and release the pungent oil, I held out a leaf to each of my sons. "Here, smell these." Now I know my children will go forward in life with an eye out for wintergreen, knowing its refreshing scent and flavor are always nearby.

Observing

Pileated Woodpecker
Dryocopus pileatus

We are going on a winter picnic. It's a bright mid-January day, and the fact that the mercury is barely above zero doesn't deter us. We won't go far. Just straight across the lake, then climb a few feet up the north-facing slope, to take a look back at the place where we live.

Eric and Todd are fitted into snowsuits, then mittened and hatted to hold off the briskness outside our sunny walls. Deb and I pull on our own snow pants, coats, hats, and mitts. The lunch of sandwiches and snacks is ready in a small pack. Outside the kitchen door, in the sheltered garage, I take down the two bright-colored plastic sleds. Settled on the snow-covered driveway, they're soon loaded up with kids and lunch. And we're off.

We skid the sleds and their cargo down the modest slope in front of the deck, out to the shore. Once we're into the open, the wind from the west makes itself known. The pressure is light, yet, at this temperature, a persistent presence that tenses up our bare faces. We wonder if we can still feel our nose tips.

We tighten up the kids' scarves, and slide on across the snow-covered ice.

Here in the open, it's all white, gray, and intense blue — the ground, the ice, the trees, the sky. There's a good six inches of snow underfoot: good going for the sleds, making the two sled-pullers tug a bit.

Crossing the lake takes only a few minutes. As we make the shore, the snow deepens, reaching up for our knees. A humped shape predicts a log below. We delve in the snow to find the bole of the fallen birch, scraping clear a spot where we four can all sit, surrounded by our lake, looking across to our own patch of woods and our home.

From here, our house looks small, a gray box perched back from the shoreline, overhung by the crowns of oak, maple, and popple. Hold your hand in front of you and it disappears, the woods becoming empty, painted in stark white. The homes of our near neighbors also look different, braced against the cold, such tiny shelters from the big outdoors. But the big outdoors is also part of home; we are here in it, the sharp-fingered breeze tingling our noses, but also telling us this is a part of the place where we belong.

Nearby, a big dead popple stub displays fist-sized cavities, a litter of toothpick-like fragments at its feet. We know it's the work of a pileated woodpecker. The big, black bird with the flaming Woody Woodpecker hairdo is not in sight today, but it cannot be far off. Perhaps it's angling in fast flight among the tree trunks, or perching on another dead trunk of its liking, hammering for access to an ant colony or tree-burrowing bugs.

Back home, the pileated has been known to perch at our feeder, a truly awkward sight, rather like a teenager attempting to ride a tricycle. The only other avian in the winter woods of the same size is the crow, never a feeder bird, so it's a bit of a shock when the woodpecker droops its wings over the feeder sides, swings its tail underneath, and somehow picks up some black sunflower seeds. When we're watching, it gives us a cold eye, mistrusting. A bird of such size must know it can command almost any situation, especially with that long, sharp beak. But it would only flee from us, trusting instead its broad, muscular wings.

We do not see a pileated this day, but we know they are near, as they do not migrate. In the spring and early summer, their hooting call will echo from back in the woods. The voice always startles; it seems out of place, as if a toucan from the rainforest has wandered here.

We munch our sandwiches, kick our feet in the dry, loose snow. The sunlight is brilliant, but the shadows, a deep, cold blue. Hot chocolate from a thermos wards off the shivers, but the house is beckoning. Soon enough we'll be trekking back across the flat white to shuck off our boots and suits, wrap the artificial heat around us, and look at winter again through a frame.

WATCHING

Northern Barred Owl
Strix varia

The voice of the owl comes from the east. It's some distance away, across the curve of the road and back in the territory where there is a little swamp. Here we can see true muskeg, a lush wetland good for a crunching walk across in the depths of winter in snowshoes. On the slopes around the swamp are some of the larger red oaks, solid citizens concealing their hollowed hearts and well-worked cavities, the doings of squirrels. In this damp spring weather, while the snow is melting, the owl likely has moved into one of these tree holes and begun its nesting program.

The who-cooks-for-you call of the barred owl comes at this time of year, and often from this part of the woods. The large birds have some privacy here and no shortage of small rodents scampering among the dry leaves from last fall.

Down by the edge of the swamp are the remains of a shack, caved-in and collapsed after years of abandonment. Walking nearby, we wonder what this place was for. The most common use of a shack in the northern woods is as a hunting shelter, the kind of rudimentary place where those out to chase deer can spend the night close to where the quarry hides. In these rough-and-tumble little buildings, wood stoves and gas lanterns set the atmosphere. Water dipped from a spring hole or melted from a snowbank and a hand-dug outhouse are all that's needed to get by. Close to the two-track road that runs around the swamp, this could have been a favorite hunting territory before the land was subdivided and sold off for housing the likes of us. It's not hard at all to imagine an old pickup or even a Model T bouncing along the little road and then pulling up by the path down to the cabin. We look and think of the hunters rising before dawn, slipping out the old door into the crisp woods and moving around the wetland, tracing the tracks that punctuate the new frosting of white.

The owls are shy and rarely seen. On one occasion, an owl found a hunting stand so good as to overcome its reticence. It was an evening like this, when the melt was not yet complete and the dark not quite set in, when the owl call came suddenly from just outside the big windows. We edged up to the glass and saw the big gray bird hunched almost at eye level, on a limb just above our hanging bird feeder. The big yellow eyes were aimed intently at the ground. We knew the seeds knocked from the feeder had attracted voles. Under the snow in the subnivean layer was a network of rodent runs; the owl was both watching and listening, with its cupped facial disk directing tiny sounds toward its ears, waiting for the moment to dive at the ground and scoop out a vole. With the feeder close by, any songbird taking the risk for a sunflower seed would be a target as well.

The night moved in, and it became too dark to see. We did not hear the owl making a sortie nor departing, and in the morning, there were no signs of a struggle in the snow. Maybe the voles had tunneled deep enough to evade the hunter.

The road by the swamp is a good place to walk for thinking, for getting off the pavement and away from even the modest human noises of the neighborhood, for looking at the big oaks on the hillsides and the crooked evergreens in the wetland. Though others must come here at times, we do not see them, so the walk here can seem like our own respite. The owls do not migrate, so they are always here as well. There is always the chance we might see the broad wings and swooping path of the solemn bird, seeking and finding what it needs for life here.

Shining

Deb walks up the road when it first warms in May, looking for new arrivals. The white trillium will swarm the woods around the bend farther east, where there is dry ground and the right mix of light and shade. They can't stay long, but when she sees them, Deb thinks of walking among them in the maple sugar bush on her home farm.

Today Eric and Todd are walking with her, keeping close eyes out for anything that's emerged. Tiny native strawberries push out at the edge of the pavement, among the earliest of the new flora. The strawberries will make miniature fruit with a big flavor. They're too good to pass up. Eric points them out to his younger brother. In a few weeks they'll be back to taste.

Black-Eyed Susan
Rudbeckia hirta

In the swamp by the curve, marsh marigolds have taken over for their month, their dark, curling leaves and bold yellow flowers roaming among the slim gray clusters of tag-alder. A few swamp buttercups are closer to the ditch line, smaller but with the same shade of yellow. Goldfinches are flying above the road, their territories already staked out and nests built. After the dull tones of the past season, any splash of color is worth pointing out. The boys skip and run, immersed in the new energy pumped in by the sunlight.

Deb loves the white daisy. Many flowers are close to her heart, but this bit of sunshine has a special place. A field of daisies is an invitation for her to run through the blossoms. The daisy was in her wedding bouquet, ringed around a centerpiece of its distant cousins, yellow chrysanthemums. The daisies are starting to rise up in the ditches, their blossom heads beginning to swell, not yet opening. Their time will come as midsummer arrives.

The white daisy is not a native. Like the equally common dandelion, they came from Europe, brought over on the early sailing ships, and found their way to this place as seeds, perhaps among grasses spread to stabilize the raw ditches when our road was first graded. Or maybe they rode along on the hooves of the dairy cattle that once grazed here or the working horses that once pulled a creaky wagon across the farm. Wherever there is disturbed ground, these plants take over. You can stand on the road, look at the tree line, and see non-natives thriving in the ditch, natives like the trillium and wood violet quietly existing in the shade beyond. If you look at the right time of year, you might see the most fragile of all, the ghost pipes with their pale, parasitic hooked stems.

Along the driveway, out by the mailbox, the daisies will co-exist with a few of their North American relation, the native black-eyed susan. The susans appear just a little later than the white daisies, orange-yellow petals circling deep brown crowns of disc florets. taking up their prominence as their cousins begin to fade. They will be with us into the cooler season that will be creeping closer every day. The time when they appear is when the weather is warmest, the skies most cloud-strewn, the wind the gentlest, and the woods most full of chlorophyll, water, and the vibrations of aliveness. Mixed with orange and yellow hawkweed, the daisies and susans will make a quilt of bright tones, calling out the warm weather and the shining days.

The black-eyed susans might be the last of the summer flowers, or the first of the fall. After they appear, it's only a matter of weeks before the blue asters, the white yarrow, and the Canada goldenrod take over the roadside. All of these aster-family plants are just waiting now, sprouting up innocuously among their earlier relatives, with their clocks set to announce their special time has come, when it comes.

It is all utterly commonplace, this random mix of plants growing at the sides of this and every road we travel in late May, in June, into July and beyond. And yet it is an event, a marvel, a powerful memory of what we know as beauty, art, what is worth enjoying in our lives. Like a stroll through a formal garden, our thoroughly informal flower show will bring us new waves of colors and arrangements in succession, as the season unfolds.

Cruising

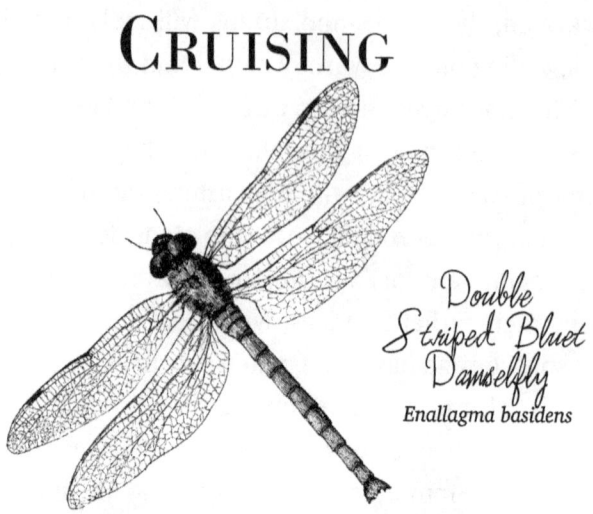

Double Striped Bluet Damselfly
Enallagma basidens

My morning paddle in the blue and white canoe can circle the lake in just a few minutes. But it's better to slow down, to look carefully at what's going on around you. Every day brings new things, takes old things away.

Gliding past the bog, with the lily pads gently tickling the canoe's chines and the redwing squawking from its tag alder branch, one can look deeply into the spaces between the green circles on the surface. Things move down there. Bugs zip about, tadpoles flutter, fish idle in the shade of the shallows. There's plenty to eat, plenty to keep the action going, and in midsummer the water is bathtub-warm.

It's a good time to be near the top of the food chain. Little things are quickly being consumed, their short lives defined by quick mating to try to keep the species going. Bigger things try to get yet bigger, to store up for their own futures, including the hard days ahead when the inevitable cold creeps back.

Past the bog, past the neighbor's dock, the south shoreline is oaks, maples, and a few surviving birch. The water's margin is grassy, with stubby, bristling reeds thrusting up. Logs sprawl into the basin, remains of trees toppled by wind. They give shelter to fish and insects, and sunning spots to the leopard frogs and the painted turtles.

A blue damselfly lights on the canoe thwart in front of me. These light-bodied flyers are out and about everywhere over the water, yet today I've not really noticed them until this moment. They're smaller and more translucent than their showier cousins, the dragonflies; perhaps that's why they're less noticed. When they land, they tuck their cellophane wings up behind, above the tail, while a dragonfly will spread out horizontally. That's how you tell them apart.

Damselflies hover like levitating needles, neon blue, red, or green, sometimes startling to the eye. Even more startling is their mating act, a kind of aerial ring-around-the-rosy that looks impossible to perform, let alone make damselfly eggs while doing it.

This is an insect we can love, not only for their aerial gymnastics, but because they do their part in the hunt for the pernicious mosquito, our most bothersome neighbor in the warm season. My damsel rests for a few of my paddle strokes, then rises and swings off toward the center of the lake, back on patrol.

The lake creates an environment that has layers both below and above the surface.

In the inch or so above the waterline, water striders and whirligig beetles thrive. Moving higher, the mosquitoes, flies, and gnats have their territory, with the dragonflies and damselflies harrying them. At head-height as I move along in my silent watercraft, the songbirds are crossing, sharing in the bounty of flying insects. Even higher, there are the raptors, hawks and eagles ready to take advantage of whatever may show weakness as it floats or swims. If we dove below the surface, we might see the swimmers, tadpoles, and skimming bugs; below them, the fish and water plants; down at the bottom, the bugs and nymphs, including the nymphs of the damselflies, hatching, hunting, and hiding until they're large enough to climb out and split their skins, then fly. The lake makes all this possible, brings abundant life into its realm.

The canoe and I swing around the western shore, in the company of dozens of damselflies, each using its multi-faceted, bulging eyes to spy out candidates for breakfast.

I wonder how I look to them, a human in a long-tailed canoe. A bit alien, I think. The feeling is mutual.

Snowing

Winterberry
Ilex verticillata

The snow started quietly, as it always does. Just a few flakes drifted, circling and wafting, in front of my windshield. A minute or two of this and it settled down to business, driven by the east wind across my route as I went north through the gut of a gray afternoon on Interstate 35. I was going home on a Thursday after four days of graduate classes in Minneapolis. Fine, damp snowflakes started to rime up on the freeway, and outside Hinckley I slowed down. There was plenty of time to finish the drive home and still take the kids around the neighborhood for Halloween "trick or treat."

Duluth and Superior huddled by the harbor, perhaps grumbling a bit about this early appearance of the imminent season. Taking it easy, I passed through southeastward, more four-lane and then the county roads, just a bit slick. Then the town roads, and I was there, turning into the garage.

Eric was home from school and Todd from day care. Deb and I soon had them costumed, and out we went into the steady, pecking snowfall. More than an inch had built up on the neighborhood driveways and porches as we walked around in the dusk, knocking on doors and collecting loot. Everyone wanted to talk about the forecast. "This might be a big one" was the message everyone had heard. Snow clung to boots and to costume parts. Other kids, passing on the road, might better have dressed as snow people or polar bears.

Friday morning, and it snowed steadily. Taking a ruler to the deck, we measured more than a foot. We went outdoors for a little snow play, but were soon back in and warming up. It looked like this was going to stay. November 1 is still quite early for serious winter, even where we live.

Saturday morning looked just like Friday, except we were approaching the two-foot mark. In front of the big windows, something was happening we hadn't imagined. The lake was getting covered up with snow. Maybe a little ice had formed, or maybe the rate of snow had surpassed the rate of melting in open water. Either way, where an open lake had been, now we looked out on a white blanket.

The TV forecasters were giddy. The end of the snowfall didn't seem to be in sight. The phenomenon was off the map; nobody had seen this kind of snow in decades. All over northwest Wisconsin and northeast Minnesota, people were snowed in, isolated. No travel was advised, and for most no travel was possible. The plows weren't out, and I trudged out to confirm the road was buried under more than two feet of untracked white.

Sunday, and it was still snowing. More than thirty inches now. We played games, watched our VHS videos, drank hot drinks, and resigned ourselves to the permanent change of season. Fall was not coming back. I forged out to the road to find a single pair of wheel tracks; someone with a big all-wheel-drive vehicle had made it in, or out. But lacking one of those, we were truly isolated.

Sunday around dinnertime, the show tapered off to a light flurry, then stopped. Monday there was no school, no work. We couldn't go anywhere, and the plow wouldn't push its way up our road until late in the day.

Among fleeting glimpses of sunshine, I scooped away almost futilely at the thigh-high drifts. A neighbor came over and helped with his snowblower, a kindness for which I'll always be grateful. The autumn shades of brown had been erased by stark white, set off by gray trunks and deep green pine boughs. Among the popples and maples along the driveway, the bright red winterberries, just ripened, caught my eye. A few pale green, fading leaves on the bushes sheltered the bold berries of this holly relative. They would be critical food for the remaining birds. They had better get them soon, I thought. It's going to be a long one.

My bet was right; it was winter from Halloween night until well into April. The big snow of 1991 is remembered across the North as the "megastorm," an intense low-pressure system that came charging out of southwest Colorado, across the plains, aimed like an avalanche at the western tip of Lake Superior. Cousin of the legendary 1940 Armistice Day blizzard, it proved again to us that powerful weather is not just an old tale. It looms just over the horizon, muttering to itself, shoving against Canadian highs and Gulf lows, waiting to suck up Lake Superior vapor and heap it on us all. We keep our boots and long johns handy, a good stock of canned goods in the basement, our ear to the wind, and our eye to the slaty clouds that slide up from the southwest when October comes back around.

LEAPING

Northern Leopard Frog
Lithobates pipiens

What could be more exciting than catching a frog? The frog at rest looks a likely target. It moves only its tiny throat, vibrating with inhales and exhales. It appears to be in a stupor, or perhaps more kindly, a frog reverie, though chances are good it's just waiting for a fly or other itinerant insect to pass within range of its sticky tongue. The common frog of our lake, the leopard, often ventures out of the water, out of the woods, and into our lawn. There it may catch the eye of one of the two small boys who roam about this area. And the pursuit begins.

    The direct approach is from the rear; step up, reach, and grab. But often the frog feels the vibrations of approaching footsteps, the breeze of reaching fingers, and launches forth with a surprisingly spry bound. Then the giggles begin, and the pounces as the startled animal makes all efforts to dodge and retreat to cover.

There are more subtle ways to capture these amphibians. Long ago I learned the hypnotic approach. You come up to the frog frontward, with small movements so as not to arouse. You present an index finger. If the frog has not sprung, you begin a circling motion with said finger, starting wide and narrowing, all the time moving the hand slowly toward the target. When your motion reaches center with your finger an inch from the frog nose, says the theory, you will have hypnotized your frog, and you can reach boldly forward to complete the capture. Sometimes this works, sometimes it doesn't.

But let's say you are successful, and your leopard frog is now nestled in your palm. You might take note of its bulging, beautiful eyes, black pupils surrounded by bright gold irises. Surely you are feeling some pressure from those surprisingly strong hind legs. The front legs, used mostly for balance, are stubby, with short digits. The frog is usually slippery, having done a good job of keeping its hide moist as all successful amphibians do. Hold it gently, but don't be surprised if it slides from your grip and you unexpectedly find yourself grasping it by the knee joints.

Leopard frog calls are more trill than croak; they're sometimes described as a snore. They call to claim their piece of the shoreline and find their mates. In our late spring evenings, the sounds from the lake and the surrounding woods become a steady vibration of frog snores.

As spring moves into summer, peepers quit, leopards call less, and the voice heard most often is that of the green frogs. These are large, robust creatures. When you catch one, you've got a handful. I haven't seen or heard any bullfrogs here, so their smaller siblings, the greens, are the top frogs. Their call is the solid "gunk!" that always seems to go with hot weather and the general lethargy that can set in with your spirit in the first week of August. Greens are big enough to eat smaller frogs and even small snakes. That would be something to see: amphibian versus reptile in a miniature re-enactment of the Triassic.

Eric and Todd love chasing the neighborhood frogs about, but they know they must be handled gently. When it's lawn mowing time, they and we are always careful to avoid frog accidents. And the frogs are very good about getting out of the way.

With their permeable skin, frogs take in a good deal of surrounding moisture, and soak up lake or river water when immersed. This high level of exposure makes them a kind of monitor for problems in the water such as pesticides and natural poisons that may come from algae blooms. And the frogs are, overall, not doing very well. Their numbers are shrinking as changes happen across their habitat.

We get so many forms of feedback from the world around us. Plants and animals thrive or shrivel; they invade new territories where their predators or competitors are absent; they reach tipping points and suddenly go extinct, as with the famous Wisconsin vanishing of the "limitless" passenger pigeon. Right now, the feedback from frogs is that some thing or things are changing in a direction that leads toward extinction. You might not miss a species or two, but in the long term, the absence of these small creatures can only bode poorly for the place we live.

On the other side of the coin, frog habitat—wetlands—

used to be considered waste land, subject to filling or draining whenever human enterprises desired. Now, many people know that a marsh or swamp is critical to many things we want: quality drinking and swimming water, reduction of waste, prevention of damaging floods, easing of the swings of drought. These are also critical to the future of frogs, and so many other living things that co-exist with us. It's rewarding to see new efforts to keep wet places wild. The voices of the frogs thank us.

GLOWING

Ghost Pipes
Monotropa uniflora

Our lives are marked by the unexpected. What is it that we remember about our pasts? We remember the things that weren't on our radar: the unanticipated and the incongruous. So it is with the ghost pipes.

I was startled when I came upon them at the edge of the woods, almost on the boundary with the paved road, just steps away from the driveway. How had I missed seeing them before? In time I decided they just hadn't been there. They don't sprout every year, only in those when conditions are just right. When they are here, they're hard to miss: their chlorophyll-free presentation sticks out among the green bushes and gray trunks on the forest floor. A place that is a little more damp is more to their liking. Yet here they are on our small patch of dry woods, glowing white and curving downward while all else is green and reaching up.

No need to strain for the sunlight; their power comes from below. They are parasites of the maples that surround them, but not direct parasites. The intermediary that produces their nourishment is a fungus. The tree and the fungus connect through the network of mycorrhizae—tiny colonies within the roots themselves. In a two-way relationship, the fungus collects and supplies moisture and minerals to the tree, receiving nutrients which it both uses and passes on the ghost pipes. The pipes receive but don't give. But I wonder if, in the long run, the fungus might bring the assets taken by the pipes back to the trees. Their decay is inevitable, their nutrients destined to filter down into the soil.

The feathery, hook-shaped plants stand out in the place where they are rooted. The low greenery around them is mostly blueberries, and it might surprise you to learn these two plants are distant cousins. Both are in the heather family—the grouping that includes many of the low-lying plants of our woods. But the evolutionary chain between these heathers is long, very long. While the blueberry is prolific, each ghost pipe lives to produce a single seed for each stalk. These seeds lay dormant, sometimes for years, until the conditions are just right. They germinate when a period of dryness is followed by a moistening, not drenching, rain. Then the seed sprouts and the pale shoots reach downward to connect with the fungus, and upward to nurture and lift the next seed for the cycle.

The patch of pipes is not large—maybe five feet in diameter. It lays almost open to the north, towards the road. Perhaps this gives them better access to moisture coming from rain or snow and unimpeded by trees. A southern exposure would serve no benefit, and might dry them out.

Ferns and bushes growing along the ditch line conceal the pipes from view. You have to know they're there to find them. You have to know the right time of year, too. Mid-June can be good for them to appear, or later in the summer if there is rain.

Eventually the pipes do dry out, shrivel, and disappear until another year when new shoots sprout.

Living things are stranger than we can imagine. What evolutionary advantage do the ghost pipes hold? What reason did they have to leave chlorophyll-based living behind? They are the exception to the rule that makes us think about the rule itself, and the processes of life that we so often take for granted.

When it comes to chlorophyll-free life, almost any piece of land will have some kind of mushroom that appears after wet weather, and dead trees everywhere are bracketed with fungi. But to host ghost pipes is special. We are lucky to have them.

SEEKING

Common Redpoll
Carduelis flammea

There are many jokes about how we northern Wisconsin residents live within close reach of the North Pole. Most people in Wisconsin have never been to this part of their own state, thinking Eau Claire and Wausau are "up north," everything beyond cold and unpredictable. Our supposedly subarctic location makes a convenient subject, an easy transition from the general discussion of weather. In conversation with a northerner, you can bring up the prospect of snow in September, the likelihood of skiing into May (it does happen), the cheap price of refrigeration when subzero temps set in, or Canadian politics. We usually play along with the gag, secretly grateful for the attention we get in the land of weather extremes.

The redpoll comes by to remind us the Arctic is really not so far away, just the flight of a small bird with a big hunger in the middle of winter. Their regular neighborhood is the boreal forest and the brushy territory that lies beyond, the dwarf birch and willow thickets that edge the stony lands by Hudson's Bay and the Coronation Gulf. When pickings are not so good in the far North, we see these tiny pale birds, with their burnt-red caps and auburn-streaked bibs, on our feeder, or more often scratching below it.

The redpoll, like all migrating birds, has a deep store of hereditary confidence built into its DNA. Sure, it's feasible there's a bird grapevine of message carriers who fly back and forth, carrying the word about conditions and provisions in far lands. But it's a better chance the potential travelers know nothing about their destination, just somehow sensing that those who have lived before have gone over that way, a thousand miles or two, and found nourishment sufficient to return. This kind of native intuition is far separated from most of the human tribe. We get a glimpse of it now and then when a tickling somewhere in our consciousness says it's time to act, perhaps on something we aren't really thinking about. But most of the time we are wrapped in layers of logic and information, prizing our facts and weighing our options, not hearing or feeling this…intuition? Something?

The redpoll has no options to weigh. When the caches of dried alder seeds are dwindling, when the temperature drops and stays down, it's go or die. It bets its remaining energy on something it cannot know or see. Its faith brings it to our feeder, where we watch it peck sunflower seeds and zoom up into the maples, just another cute little finch.

The redpoll is joined at the feeder by our resident black-capped chickadees and red-breasted nuthatches, plus a small air force of other migrants: grosbeaks, finches, dark-eyed juncos. Bird feeding as a human intervention has its effects and is really a conceit, something we do to entertain ourselves.

Science tells us the birds don't need it; neither do they especially become dependent and starve if we can't fill the feeder or if we abandon it for a Mexican vacation in midwinter. But seeing the redpoll and its compadres there on a subzero winter morning is an object lesson. We, too, take chances, get hungry, and act with blind faith on something we just can't explain, even to ourselves. But things usually turn out all right, as right as they are for a small bird in a strange land with a full belly and a long spring trip ahead.

Rising

Canada Mayflower
Maianthemum canadense

My mushroom anchor spends most of its days napping under a good-sized red oak close by the shore. I found it in my father's boat shop many years ago, back in a corner with some other odds and ends, dock leg brackets and battered old green oars. It had already been there a long time, a relic of when he did more business in the things needed for outfitting boats: life jackets and cleats and motor mounts, lights and anchors. I asked if I could have it, and, with a positive response, it moved to my shoreline. There it gets put to use when we go out in the canoe to fish. Hitched to a thwart, then dropped into the warm, dark lake, it keeps us from drifting out of place and into the bait-tangling weeds.

The place where it rests when not in the water is a mossy patch. When the snow goes, it's a good spot to watch for one of the earliest signs of the green-up. After several warm days, the crisp leaves of the Canada mayflower poke upward out of the moss. Their curled shapes surround the anchor and even shoot up through its drain holes. Our season is here, they say. With luck, it may even be the month of May.

Canada mayflowers edge the portage trails in the Boundary Waters Wilderness, not too far to the north, and are abundant in the boreal woods beyond, the great spruce woods of Canada. They occupy the firm land surrounding boggy patches everywhere in the North, including our neighboring bog. Their bright green jumps out in the woods, asserting their belonging in a plant community that includes the bluehead lily, bunchberry, wintergreen, mosses, and, rare but always welcome, the ladyslipper. These plants grow where it's dry, but near soft and wet, close to a bog or a lake.

The mayflower does have a blossom, a modest spiky thing with tiny white bells on it. It hardly draws notice. The leaves are what make the mayflower plant stand out in the woods. Turgid is a powerful, guttural word, telling the strength of internal pressures that come up from the roots, up with the water that wants so much to evaporate into the sky, up and into the channels and cells of the leaf of the mayflower. The turgid, pointed leaves have an incredible push behind them. I've seen them punch holes in the dry, red-brown fallen oak leaves here on the moss. Like us, they want the sun, they need the sun, and there is so little time for it.

The green of the mayflower leaves is the strongest shade of chartreuse, a spring color that cannot be denied, though it be dashed by cold rain and sprinkled with sleet. When the mayflower is up, things have melted, and they will keep on melting. You can take it to the bank.

The green comes in bright patches, scattered about near the lakeshore, under the trees. The plant has small red berries later in the season, but its main way of moving is through underground rhizomes, spreading out beneath the duff, building its safety in numbers. The deer will munch at these patches, enjoying a crisp young salad as a relief from their winter dinner of hazel twigs. There will be more fresh, crunchy shoots of other species coming up soon in the nearby bog. In just a few days, all these fresh greens will give does strength for the birthing of fawns, perhaps while lying near the water on a bright chartreuse carpet, the comfort of the forest floor.

Floating

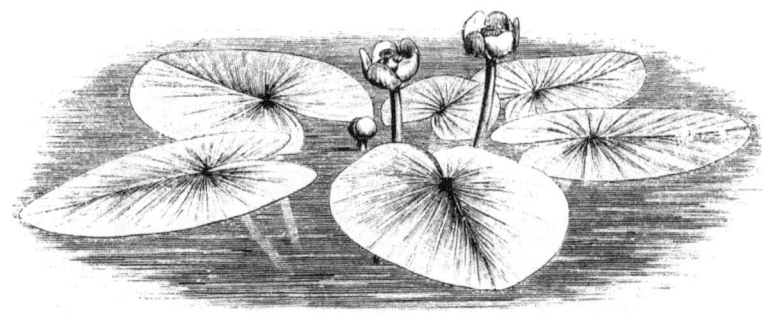

Yellow Pond-Lily
Nuphar variegata

Deb and I lift the canoe out from under the big oak and carry it the few steps over to the vee in our weedy shoreline where we launch. Our life-jacketed children are waiting, with only a smidgen of patience. Eric climbs in over the gunwale and makes his seat on a boat cushion in front of me. Todd gets a boost and is soon stationed behind his mother. I lift the stern, slide the watercraft forward, step in, find my balance. I sit and take my first paddle stroke.

The lily pads whisper against the canoe's waterline. We push out through the few yards of their habitat, out to the deeper part of the lake. As we reach the line where the lilies taper off, we turn left and paddle the edge of the emergent plants. It's a sunny early-summer day. The pads have been up from the bottom only a few weeks. Now their fresh, verdant green leaves lie spread, soaking up energy.

I enjoy my solo paddles but also the family trips we take around the bowl of the lake. It's a good way to spend time and together sense what's going on here in our neighborhood.

The water is open where we move slowly and in near-silence, so navigating strokes are minimal. To our right, the sparkling view across to the bigger woods to the south, to the homes of several neighbors peeking out on the west side. To our left, the shoreline, with plenty of chances to see birds, bog plants and flowers, zooming dragonflies and maybe a turtle on a log. And between us and the shore, the expanse of lilies.

Flapped a bit by the breeze, the pond-lilies blanket the shoreline waters. We know there are frogs in there, and the kids are keeping a sharp eye out for them. Speckled leopard frogs and shiny green frogs live here in good numbers. They hide under the pads, with their smooth, rounded snouts protruding, just enough to get air and flick out a sticky tongue when a flying snack cruises past. They often squirm a bit when our wake lifts them, trying to keep position. It's not hard to see them. It's harder to catch them, so today we're letting them live their froggy lives undisturbed.

The two kinds of prevalent surface insects, water striders and whirligig beetles, maneuver the spaces between the lilies. The whirligigs are our favorites; they twirl so swiftly and numerously, it's hard to follow the path of just one beetle. Their scientific name, Gyrinidae, really tells what they're all about: gyration. Their action is about predator avoidance and maybe also pursuit of smaller creatures that provide their dining. Close watching of the Gyrinidae might reveal their complex social behaviors. Bunches of them do a dance that brings hunters among them to the outside, while more placid, satiated, and vulnerable dancers glide inward. They may seem permanently immersed, but as beetles they have fully functional wings and can fly out of the reach of attackers if needed. I've never noticed them flying, though. How do they keep from getting cross-eyed and dizzy? Eric and Todd would like to know.

The skittish striders are showing off the uncanny properties of water surface tension. Their skating ability is unmatched by any other fauna we see. While they have a mosquito-ish look to them, they are true bugs; you can call them a bug and be correct in your terminology. The trick of their water-walking has to do with the spread of their legs, the tiny hairs on their appendages, and the propulsion system; the middle legs do the work of moving forward, the long back legs support and steer. The third set of legs have claws for puncturing their prey, which is other insects that fall into the water. Feeding involves using sharp mouth-parts to suck out the juices. These tiny creatures have voracious habits.

As we swing along the bog, the redwing who lives there flutters up into the tag-alder bush near the center of the wetland. We love to hear its "konk-a-ree" trill; when first heard each year, it means spring. Now we move past the bog edge. Sweet gale is showing its brownish catkin blossoms, and a few pinkish-white flowers of bog rosemary can be spotted among them.

Past the neighbor's dock and on along the south shore is the most mature forest of the shoreline. Popple logs lay in the water, extending off the bank, knocked down by thunderstorms or soggy snowfalls. Between them are the lily pads, and together with the smaller leaves of watershield, they provide cover for fish, frogs, and bugs. Shorelines that look neat and free of such messy obstacles provide much less diverse habitat. We're lucky that the lake has this long southern stretch of undeveloped land. It's owned by a neighbor who lives high up on the ridgeline and leaves their shore to nature.

Eric is looking intently into the water. Is he watching for

fish or something unknown down there? My older son has a good eye already for natural features, for the things that move and shape our community here. He would probably like to trail a hand in the water, to get the feel of it. I wouldn't object, though Deb might get concerned for his safety. But for now, he's content to look and listen.

Todd and Deb are having a conversation. It might be about mosquitos, of which there are a few cruising out over the shoreline. None of us is a great fan of this annoying flyer, so eager to go for any exposed skin. I paddle a little harder, hoping to move us past this spot where it's notably buggy.

In the southwest corner of the lake, a mad collection of logs and lily pads lie in shallow mucky water. There are more bugs here, not fewer. A few flies join the party. We brush them off before they have a chance to bite.

We take a sharp right turn, give a push with the paddles, and soon cruise past a fringe of cattails growing just before we pass our two near neighbors. The breeze from the west picks up a bit, and the biting insects are left behind. Now we slip again through the fringe of lily pads, moving the canoe's bow up onto the weedy shore. Our paddle around the lake has taken less than fifteen minutes, but it was enough to give us new things to think and talk about. As days, months, and years pass, we hope our children will gain the patience to spend more time finding out about the great abundance, the shimmering life that lives in the water.

Clinging

Little Brown Bat
Myotis Lucifugus

Eric, Todd, and I are building a bat house. We have a simple set of plans and some leftover boards from the house construction. The plans are rather like those for a wood duck house, but smaller, a vertical shape with a slanted roof. And there is no hole for access. Instead, the bottom of the house is left open, and a couple of baffles separate the space. The idea is that the bats fly up underneath, squeeze into one of the exposed slots, clamber upward, hook their claws into the baffle or sidewall, and enjoy sweet dreams—in the daytime, of course, since bats are notoriously nocturnal.

We work out in the garage, near the gaping open door. It's only taken a few saw cuts to turn our rough boards into sides, roof, and baffles. Now I'm using screws to assemble the structure.

Deb comes by and examines the project. "Don't you need something for the bats to hold onto?" I figure they wedge in there and get a good toehold, but she might have a point. Completing the process is delayed until we have a trip into town. There, I pick out some kind of plastic screen that I can staple to the interior surfaces. Can't have bats dropping out of their safe spots during a batly snoozefest.

When all is ready, we secure the house to a mid-sized popple not far from the deck, lashing it on with surplus electrical wire. Bat housing is now open for business, and we keep an eye out for occupants.

We were motivated to build this bat condo by our recent visit to Stockton Island in the Apostle Islands National Lakeshore. After packing our tents and sleeping bags, we made the hour-and-a-half drive to the waterfront in Bayfield, the most picturesque town on all of the south shore of Lake Superior. We went to the Pier Plaza, overlooking the harbor, for lunch. There I experienced the most incredible slice of banana cream pie I have ever encountered; the taste buds still salivate at the memory of it. After leaving the car in the overnight lot, we strapped on our backpacks and boarded the Island Princess, the watercraft that doubles as both cruise boat and camper shuttle to the Lakeshore's largest campground.

As we motored out of the Bayfield harbor, I noticed the old tour boat Chippewa lashed to the dock. Back in the 1960s, as a young boy, my family and I rode the chugging Chippewa's route out past Basswood, Hermit, and Oak Islands to Rocky Island, where we docked by a small restaurant and snack bar. The pie there was not an amazing banana cream, but it was sweet and satisfying after the Chippewa's languid passage along the sharp-edged sandstones of the inner islands.

Here with Deb and the kids on the Island Princess, which planes rather than chugs, nonetheless it was more than an hour before we passed the outermost point of Madeline and motored beyond to the dock at Presque Isle Point. The view southward across the mouth of Chequamegon Bay took in waves, gulls, boats, clouds, far-reaching islands, and beyond, the Penokees and Porkies, ranges of rolling hills on the mainland. We and the other campers hitched up our gear, while day trippers stepped off to walk the "singing sands" of nearby Julian Bay. The sands don't really sing, but they do squeak in a unique tone, thanks to granular friction.

During our two-night stay at Campsite 3, we also trekked the singing sands, hiked the swamp boardwalk where we saw an amazing number of garter snakes, and picked blueberries for our breakfast cereal behind the beach. The National Park Service ranger came around with wild cranberries he had found in the recesses of the bog. And we availed ourselves of his evening ranger programs, just a short walk up the trail in the amphitheater. This is where we received our bat orientation.

Just before dusk, the ranger entertained us with the tales of the lives of the bats around us. We learned how they voraciously vacuum up our pests, the ever-annoying mosquitoes. We learned how they sleep away their days wedged into narrow places: loose spots in the popple bark, tree crotches and cracks, small openings in cabins. We learned our bats were declining, perhaps because these crevices in their habitats were becoming more scarce. And we learned how bat houses can help give them the private resort they need to survive.

As the denouement, the ranger snapped on the volume of the bat signal receiver, sitting on the nearby wall. The voicings of the circling winged rodents squeaked out of the little speaker. We were absorbed, trying to synchronize the sound with the swoop of the creatures we could now see passing above us.

We went home on the Island Princess, did our part, built our bat house. While everything was done according to plan, I don't think any of us can testify that we ever saw a bat come to, or go from, the house. No matter. The bats were there, as we could plainly see when we sat into deep dusk on the deck, spotting their paths through the canopy of hardwood branches above us. I doubt it really mattered to them if we were there or not. Yeah, we had cut down some of their popples and replaced them with a small, odd-shaped box of a place they might or might not have liked to squeeze into. But the mosquitos were always there, and that was enough. Migrating animals, they would spend the warm days in our neighborhood, making the outdoors more comfortable for us while satisfying their appetites. Then they would junket off to Texas, or beyond, when the days turned short and the skeeters scarce.

INVESTIGATING

Black-capped Chickadee
Poecile atricapillus

Aldo Leopold loved the chickadee. You picture him in the yard of his Southern Wisconsin shack on a spring day, cupping the tiny bird in a palm as he grips the banding tool. It pecks at his hand and squirms a bit as the metal is crimped around a leg but soon is back on a maple twig above, probing at its new decoration. The sun brightens, and he is swinging off across the rustling cattail marsh, dog loping at his side.

We are in the land of the deer, the land of the squirrel and of the frog and crow, but more than all this, we are in the land of the chickadee. They flit energetically across the yard and around the house, masters of the airspace at six feet above ground. Surely their nests are close by, but hidden inside a tree cavity or old woodpecker hole, so never seen. Their calls are all around us. At the feeder they chatter, conversing in some intense way about who goes next and the quality of the sunflower morsels.

On damp, dripping days when the snow starts to sink, the two-note call of chickadees echoes across the woods and down by the lake. I whistle back and hear a bird reply. It may just be an illusion, but I think we have a talk before we each go our way.

We know this of the language of the chickadee: when it calls out its name, chick-a-dee-dee-dee, the number of dees relates to the amount of danger it senses around it. More dees means a bigger threat has been spotted, maybe a raptor or owl in sight and moving toward the flock. Warnings go up, and the birds scatter. Tucked under a bristling branch in the conifers, their favorite tree, they quickly vanish.

A chickadee never lacks curiosity, nor an appetite. As we have lunch on the deck on a warm day, birds perch on the railing just a few feet from our elbows. If we sat perfectly still, they might land on our plates to pick up the sandwich crumbs. They tote the feeder seeds away and hide them in crevices or under loose bark on a dead popple. When things get lean later on, they'll be back for their sustenance.

Out in front of the deck, the feeder is their territory unless a bigger, aggressive bird such as a bluejay shows up. Even then, they swoop in, a constant reminder that it's time to fill up and move along, buddy. When I fill the feeder and go to re-hang it, sometimes a chickadee will be perched on it before I can finish the job. There's not a lot of room for patience in those tiny bodies.

Eric and Todd make bird feeders, Cub Scout projects involving cutting into milk cartons and folding out flaps, punching sturdy wire through the top. They scoop seeds in, and we hang the feeders from the maple branch just a few feet from their windows. Soon Eric is back: "There's a bird in my feeder!" We watch the black-caps flit back and forth, swinging down out of the taller branches above to snatch the prize, then just as quickly disappear again up into the forest.

They are year-round residents and owners of the place. We see them all the time, hardly notice them, rarely give their presence a thought. Yet they must know so much we don't: where there are good places to hide food, which trees are best for nesting, which direction the hawks come from, what noises can be ignored, and what must be checked out. They live about six years, so generations of chickadees are passing around us as we live our days in their view. For all their tribe, we carry what we think is the same affection Leopold had, the feeling of brightness that comes when we hear their chatter across our woods.

Towering

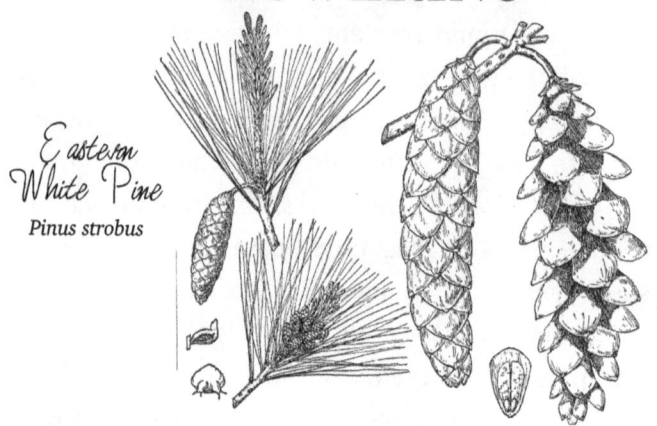

Eastern White Pine
Pinus strobus

There are two pines. One reaches out over the road from its place next to the driveway. When we came it was short enough that I could tip up a ladder and string it with colored lights in December, but a few years have passed, and it now reaches up more than twenty feet. The other, perhaps forty or fifty years old, stands by the shoreline. It's a tad twisted in the branches, not quite the classic beauty yet. But give it another half a century, and it will climb above its neighbors, spreading out its crown to take on its true role, king of the forest.

Across the lake are trees already in the mature adult stage, stately and windswept, gracing the skyline. Look at them, and you see a glimpse of the old Pinery, the great stands that once greened the valleys of the Wisconsin, the Chippewa, the nearby Brule. Solid, gray trunks go up and up, unbroken by branches for forty, fifty, sixty feet. Near the eastern North American coast, such trees were prized for masts of sailing ships. Marked with the king's brand, they were forbidden to be cut for any other use.

The story of the great clearcut is well known here. Our tall virgin pines were hand sawed with a long, bendy crosscut, skidded behind oxen, and floated south. After the rush through the foaming rapids, they would be run through the mills and come out as yellow planks, raw material for a million barns and prairie houses. When it all was gone, our forebears stood stunned, wondering how it could be over so quickly. Most thought it could never return. We don't have the great clusters of trees that once stood along our waterways, nor the giants that the arms of three loggers could not span. But the pines have come back in many spots, like this one overlooking the southwest shore. Here they lean outward, probing the sky and the wind.

On a bright summer day, I heard loud, grating cries from the crowns of the pines across the lake to the southwest. The racket went on for a while, then three young bald eagles came flapping out of the high branches. The big, brown birds circled upward, then dove and dodged at each other. I can't say whether a family dispute was underway, or if it was just eagle play, but it was good to see the great birds using the pines for perch and shelter. Over on the Brule, canoeists often spot a looming nest, sixty or more feet above the valley floor, locked in sturdy pine branches. When it comes to staying up out of the reach of predators, the eagle knows the value of a solid white pine.

Visit the pine on a warm summer day to find its real character, that of a living community. Bees and other flying insects will be working its flowers and cones. Bugs of all kinds scuffle up and down the trunk. There will be birds: pine grosbeaks perhaps, or the ever-present chickadees that shelter among its clumps of needles. There could be a pine martin up there, ready to chase the red squirrel up and down the gray, somber trunk.

I wish I could come back in a hundred years to see our two pines. The one near the road is a little close. Its proximity to the blacktop might become a problem. The other, though, has nothing to worry about, save the kind of powerful windstorms that sometimes rake our country when the cool arctic jet stream and the warm, wet Gulf air collide here. With shallow roots and the leverage of a lofty top, a few pines become tip-ups, laying down their trunks, raising a curve of soil and tangled roots up above head height. I'd rather dream, though, of our middle-aged pine as a future giant, standing out over its lesser neighbors, spreading tall green out over the glittering shallows at its feet.

CONVERSING

American Crow
Corvus brachyrynchos

By the side of the garage, I clip into the Salomon bindings of my new, black Finnish-made Peltonen skis. It's flat light today, the sky a shade of concrete. The snow around me reflects the sky's bland tone. The house siding beside me is pale, like the surrounding trunks of popples with their angular black markings. The world is monochrome, and so am I, in black pants, jacket, and hat. Just a bit of raspberry color on my ski boots interrupts the scene. I could bury my ankles in the fine powder of yesterday's snowfall and disappear.

Bumping over the driveway snowbank and onto the lake path, I make my way down to the shore, turning my skis to the snowplow stance to control my speed. In mid-January, the frozen plane of the lake is almost pristine, an unmarked canvas. My goal today is to write long, jagged stripes on it with my gliding apparatus.

Cross-country skiing came into this territory a hundred years ago with the Finns, Swedes, and Norwegians who cleared the forests and glided along their fence lines on days like this.

It was a utility, not really a sport, just a way to get into the back forty. That all changed in 1973 when Tony Wise thought up an audacious race, a thirty-mile trek between his two tourist attractions, up the Namekagon valley from Historyland in Hayward to Mount Telemark outside Cable. The American Birkebeiner demonstrated the emerging ski technologies brought over from Europe: lighter and stronger skis, purpose-made boots, more efficient waxing, a better understanding of the movements of skiing on the flats and the uphills. Soon my father ran a few pairs of old wood downhill skis through a table saw to narrow them, screwed on Rottefella three-pin bindings from Norway, and started our family on a long journey into the x-c world. It's that journey I'm continuing today.

Moving out onto the lake surface, I pass the small rink I've shoveled for Eric's and Todd's enjoyment. Here we like to skate around a bit, sometimes play some goal-free pond hockey. Eric has joined a nearby youth program, one where outdoor ice is still the rule, where parents flood the rink on brisk evenings and handle the rudimentary tractor-pulled ice surfacer.

I set my poles, step forward, and start to move into the rhythm. I decided last year to switch from the traditional striding technique into the faster skating method of skiing. I'm working on the weight transfer and balance. The first thing to learn is to commit to the gliding ski, to step confidently from one to the other. I'm still subconsciously ambivalent, still used to keeping my feet under me as I did in the classic striding stance. Today will be another self-taught lesson.

I move around the lake clockwise, following the shore. Several inches of loose powder make me push. The first circuit will be the hardest, then my own tracks will ease the tug at my feet.

It takes about five minutes to go around. It's quiet out here. Not the slightest wind. No cars on the road. No kids in the snow-shrouded yards, nor on the ice. Then, as I finish my first go-around, I notice the crows flying to the big oak down by our landing. They land, flutter wings, then set a raucous call echoing across the basin. In a moment, a response comes from the south, over toward the other lake there. I ski on and think about the crow conversation going on around me.

Crows are known to be among the most intelligent animals. You hear stories of pet crows, tamed and taught to do tricks, seen in northern Wisconsin barrooms. And their vocabulary is deep. When you hear liquid gurgling, or soft, throaty mutterings, the meaning must be much different from the racket we usually associate with their voices.

I wonder today if the crows are discussing me. Certainly there's not much else moving in the neighborhood to hold their attention. Nesting is long over, mating not quite yet on the agenda. They might like to spy some roadkill or a place to scrape out some acorns, but there's not much around for them. Despite their omnivorous diet, winter can be slim crow pickings.

So it's intriguing to have an audience high above me. I make the second loop; yes, it's much easier going. I'm starting to sweat just a little in my fleece top and nylon pants. Though the temperature is in the low twenties, it's comfortable. I feel like I belong out here. I hope the crows are agreeing.

There is a swing to the skate-ski technique. You learn to move smoothly, spending about the same amount of time on each ski. It's a workout; I'm starting to breathe more heavily, feeling the energy go out through my legs to the skis, through my arms to the poles. Sometimes it feels as if you get a little spring from the tensioned fiberglass under your heels. Any edge, any bonus helps when you have many kilometers to go.

I start to examine the snowy surface around me. Deer tracks, of course. A few people-tracks, leading out from the houses around the lake. A few unidentified dents in the powder. Maybe they're crow tracks.

After five trips around, I've made a track that allows me to ski at almost my best. A firm trail with groomed corduroy, long grooves in the snow, is the ultimate, but the lake is a reasonable facsimile for today. I could use some hills, though. The Birkie is notorious for its thirty miles of up-and-down. The course as we'll ski it this year is a net descent of several hundred feet, but I'll have to climb hundreds and hundreds of feet to finish it. Skiing uphill might seem contrary, but it's the secret of the skating technique: you can glide up. All it takes is stamina... stamina that I currently lack.

Ten times around now. Starting to feel it in the calves, in the thighs. Tired yet? Yes, a little. I shouldn't be. When I finish up, I'll have gone around twelve times and traveled about five miles. That would be one-sixth of the Birkie's thirty-mile distance.

I think I'll do fifteen times around today. The crows have left, flying off northward over the house, toward the hill and the bigger lake beside it. With ice fishing going on, maybe a few stunted panfish or leftover minnows will be on the ice, for pickings. Or maybe it's just a better show over there.

Delighting

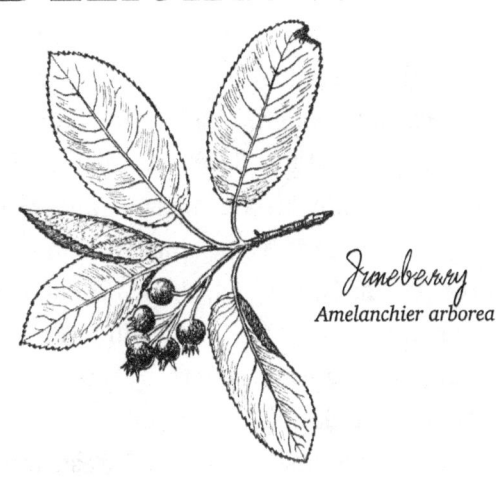

Juneberry
Amelanchier arborea

My grandfather's cabin looks out from a steep bank above a lakeshore in the Harrison Hills not far from Rhinelander, a good two hundred miles east and a bit south from here. The small cottage, painted barn red with white-trimmed windows, tells of its Swedish heritage. Deb and I saw many like it when we drove up the west side of Lake Vänern to the hill country north of Karlstad. There we found the shelving rock on the shore of Lake Borssjön where a young man, my great-great-grandfather Nils Nilsson, stepped out of his family's rowboat on Sundays and walked up the slope to a red-painted church.

In the Harrison Hills, the way to the lake is down a curving stairway of sturdy concrete blocks. My father and his high school buddies, Don and Kurt and Roy and Delos, set them into the hillside while building the cabin. It was right after World War II, an event in which several of them saw more of the world than they could have imagined as children. In my mind, I can see them in t-shirts and khakis, hammering, sawing, and shoveling while working on brown bottles of Schoen's Old

Lager from Wausau, sharing yarns of the Philippines and the liberation of Europe.

Down at the foot of the block stairs, just above the stony shoreline, a juneberry bends over the path from the right. When I had grown tall enough, I could reach up and grab a handful of the dark red and purple fruits, tasting of their bland juice and the almond hint in the seeds. Grandpa and I agreed they weren't nearly as good as the sharp-flavored raspberries picked down the Ament Lake Road, then sprinkled over Rice Krispies when the sun came in the front windows. Still, the juneberry was a fruit, and it grew wonderfully free, right here by our path to the boat and a day of chasing pike.

Now, at our home in the northwest, the path to the lake takes off from the deck stairs and leads down through the moist woods to the marshy shoreline. It brings memories of portage trails in the Boundary Waters Wilderness, a way through the trees to the place where the gleam of blue water promises. At the end, just before the iris and reeds, a juneberry leans over the path from the right.

In the right season, the dark-red and purple fruit are there, ready to evoke a childhood memory. What once seemed bland now brings a delicate fruitiness and a hint of their rose heritage. They might make a fine jelly, dark red with that touch of almond essence.

While the juneberry is a humble, low, curving tree, it comes from a hardy and widespread line that roams all over the northern cap of the planet. Its genus name *Amelanchier* is what it's called in France, with roots going back to the Celtic. On the prairie, the saskatoon is a juneberry, and in the subarctic, the serviceberry is our friend by another name. I knew the low-growing shadbush for many years before I learned it was just a nickname for a young juneberry. Had I looked closely in central Sweden, I'm sure *Amelanchier* was there, bending out among the willows below the red pines.

The juneberry owns another melodic name, amygdaloid. I met this word on the map of Isle Royale, where Amygdaloid Island stands just offshore to the northwest, a narrow strip of old lava covered with spruce and scrub, home to a National Park ranger station. Its name is a geologic term for cavities in the basalt at its foundation, yet amygdaloid also means "a stone fruit." Somewhere among the evergreens, a juneberry bush or two is likely to be hiding.

The best gift of the juneberry may be something other than the fruit. When the snow is gone at last, its blossoms are the first tree flowers we see. Another juneberry grows next to our storage shed. It curves and arches, natural art like the centerpiece in a Japanese garden. For an achingly short few days each May, it graces the yard with white loveliness, a clear sign we have entered the heart of springtime.

HOPPING

American Toad
Anaxyrus americanus americanus

Often I wonder what it is to be *hyla crucifer*, the peeper, the first voice of spring. When a good foot of solid ice and three feet of snow seal up the swamps and shorelines, the hyla is there, snuggled in chilled mud, waiting it out. Peepers exist in blind faith for the coming day when the sun gets the upper hand, the ice dissolving. The next day, it seems, they are out in full voice, announcing to all that a new regime is coming in. April 15th is a pretty good average date here for their appearance, brightening the tax deadline a bit; maybe that explains the bold X they carry on their backs, like a mark on a federal form. They will be joined in a moment by wood frogs, chorus frogs, mink frogs. Then later, leopards and greens.

The raucous froggy voices of the warming months echo across the evening woods and through the night, each in its turn and season. Eventually the goals of mating are accomplished, and the calls of the early frogs die away. Taking their place is a steady, businesslike trill. When we hear the high-pitched buzz, we know the toads are out, the last voice of the spring season. They sing just about the time the blackberries blossom, last of the wild fruits. What they're saying is "goodbye to spring; this is summer."

I learned to recognize the voice of the toad and the other Anuran calls while studying herpetology at the University of Wisconsin's Pigeon Lake Field Station, twenty-some miles to the southeast of here. With our professor, we band of students roved the national forest and surrounding lands, helping out with amphibian research. Toting a bulky battery-powered reel tape recorder with a microphone on a stick, we splashed into the shallow, sandy lakes on evenings to first record each frog's call, then capture the caller to note vital physical characteristics. This style of frog-catching features the thrill of the hunt, the excitement of the grab, the comedy of the regular misses, and the farce of the complete collapse into the shallows. We were well entertained during our three weeks of study.

After the trilling season, the toads are quiet and not much seen, unless you bump into one scrabbling solemnly along, poking out a route through last year's leaves in the dry woods. Egg laying, hatching, and life as a tadpole pass mostly unnoticed.

Emergence and migration can be another matter. On an August morning, the yard is suddenly busy with hopping action. Tiny toads, less than an inch long, are working their way uphill, out of the lake, and toward the higher ground. In the dozens they move along in cohort, spread apart but clearly sharing motivation. Eric and Todd are fascinated by this toad expedition, especially since the migrants are easy to pick up and study. The morning passes, and they are gone, hiding in the woods and across the road. The next generation might be here again when August comes around, or it may be several years before we again see the march of the toad horde.

The toad, of course, is our great friend. Anyone who eats insects is welcome in the neighborhood, with attention to the mosquito especially prized. Their bumbling progress through the ground cover reminds us of their old name, *Bufo*, given to them by the Romans, with an appropriate hint of the clownish in it. Yet the toad is stolid and serious, firm about its needs and purposes. Only when it wakes in the late spring woodland and sends out its trill do we hear the music in its heart.

Adopting

Red-winged Blackbird
Agelaius phoeniceus

I have been thinking about the notion of lakeshore ownership. While real estate ads might wax sentimental about "owning your own frontage," and the county Register of Deeds holds a document showing our possession of title, it seems to me we are not owners of our shore but rather residents within a community that, at best, co-exists with us. This boundary meeting of water and gravelly earth, richly stocked with life in many shapes, is something we can never reasonably understand, let alone manage or claim to own. Even the term stewardship seems a little presumptuous. We are able to live here, and the myriad of life around us has shifted to accommodate our presence. It continues to shift and adjust, depending on the pressure we place on the land, the trees and plants, and the wildlife.

We like to think we have minimized some of our larger impacts. Use of water might be the most significant. We are on an isthmus between two lakes, a narrow ridge of land about 600 feet wide. The road runs down the center, with most of the lots on each side occupied either by full-time homes or seasonal cabins. There are a dozen of these along the length of the isthmus, about a third of a mile. Each of us has our own well for water supply, and each of us has our own septic system.

The state and county have standards for placement of the wells and particularly for layout and separation of the septic systems, which process wastewater back into the water table. Septic systems that move waste toward lakes and streams have a heightened risk of sending chemicals and pollutants into the surface water. Somewhat to our surprise, we found that the terrain of our location allowed us to direct the septic system away from the lake. Instead, it runs parallel to the center of the isthmus, yet still downhill— you always want it running downhill—as our property slopes away from the glacial ridge to our northeast. Whatever happens underground is never fully known, but we rest easier knowing we're not piping our wastewater toward the lake.

We are fortunate to live in an area of abundant groundwater, unlike many other parts of our nation. The driller who came to put in our well looked up the slope of the isthmus, then turned and looked the other way. "I put in that one, and we got good water at eighty feet," he said, nodding toward our downhill neighbor's home. "And that one up there was eighty-four. I expect we'll find your water at about eighty-two." And that's exactly where he struck it.

Solid waste disposal, however, is required to be a thoroughly urbanized procedure. Our county has a contract to have all solid waste trucked to the big Superior landfill, a steadily growing mountain of stuff heaped close, perhaps too close, to the Lake Superior shoreline. At least we're fortunate to have a good recycling program, which we diligently use. And we look forward to the day when those mountainous landfills are mined for their rich collections of metals, and their other content is used to produce energy.

We have chosen not to exercise our ability to clear a forty-foot corridor between house and lake and landscape it as we might please. We know that maintaining the natural shoreline vegetation is good for the lake and all the life around it. It filters runoff, hosts complex systems of food and shelter, and provides some protection from heavy weather. It also continues a passageway around the shoreline for many small animals. The narrow path we take to the water has minimal impact, and, with the leaves gone half the year, we do get our view of the lake.

Our yard is small, extending only a dozen or so feet from the walls of the house. On the north side, where I sometimes have my garden, there is more open space, but we need that for room to let the kids run. Our graveled driveway and the space occupied by the house itself are the remainder of our impact on the property.

We've planted vegetation around the house that has its impacts. Some is native, such as blueberries and iris. Others, like the barberry bush by the deck, are not resident here but grow elsewhere in North America. And some, like hostas and primroses, are non-natives. We've been careful to choose species that don't aggressively escape the garden and become troublesome invasives.

Of course, we use energy—electricity—and generate heat that works its way out into the larger environment. The house is insulated as well as we could make it to reduce our energy use. Our choice of electric heat ensures that our production comes from a central plant, not far away, that uses sawdust and waste wood while its emissions are carefully controlled. We think it's more efficient, with less impact on the atmosphere, than burning wood or fossil fuels in our house.

These are the things we've been able to manage. Our commute to work, our travels for recreation, our choices of the things we buy, the materials we used to build, equip, and decorate our house, the expense of bringing our food here—this and more could be measured, added up, and figured into our budget of impacts on the planet. Yet we know the final sum: it costs the planet to have us here. We minimize the costs we can, accept the ones we can't, and hope the larger budget of humanity might someday reach a point of sustainability.

Back at the water's edge, we look out on the lake with confidence that it belongs, not just to the shoreline owners, but to all of us. Wisconsin's Public Trust Doctrine, recorded in our state constitution, gives ownership of all navigable waterways to the citizens of the state. While not directly mentioned, there are many other stakeholders implied in this public ownership: owners with fins, claws, and wings, with leaves and blossoms.

Perhaps, at best, we should think of ourselves as adopters. For better or worse, this 0.69 acres of the planet has been placed in our care. We're free to use immense power on it, to change it forever. We're free to leave it just as it is. Since we are living here, we have chosen a middle way. But we challenge ourselves to stay closer to the way it is, the way natural processes have made this shoreline.

As I think about who might be the owners of this place where we are resident, the red-winged blackbird in the bog comes to mind. This lively, aggressive bird is always speaking to us as we paddle out into our public waterway. It moves from shrub to shrub, observing our actions, seemingly seeking reassurance we won't impact the environment it needs. To see a red-wing chase crows and larger birds away from its nesting grounds is to feel courage, determination, and risk of self for the greater good: the future of the species, or at least the clutch of eggs below. The red-wing knows it belongs here, as did its forebears, and as will those who come after it, as long as it does its part. It's good to live in a place where such neighbors are all around us.

BRANCHING

Staghorn sumac
Rhus typhinia

The small clump of sumac beside the entry to the driveway always makes me smile when I look it over. Flooding back are memories of the place I lived when small, a territory of fields, pastures, and airy woodlands. Great thickets of sumac stood at the boundaries, edging the woods where we local kids played and roamed for hours. Hard to penetrate, these bushy strongholds grew with vigor, spreading through their rhizomes into the edges of the grazing lands. If you did shove your way inside, pressing through the bending stalks, you might find something special. An opening in the center of the patch could be your private fort, your place of concealment and quiet when you wanted time away from your compatriots in the woods. Writer Jessamyn West knew about these secret sumac openings and wrote one into her novel *The Massacre at Fall Creek* as a trysting place for lovers. We were far too young for an interest in romance, but we were always ready to explore the emerging mysteries just beyond our backyards.

The sumac is in a diverse and wide-ranging family, the Anacardiaceae. The marquee member is the cashew tree, and you will also find here the pistachio and mango. Poison sumac is in there too, though not closely related nor found in our neighborhood, but poison ivy is another cousin and turns up near stream banks here.

The curving trunks of sumac make it easy to guess where the name staghorn comes from. The gray, forked stalks hold up the mattes of compound leaves, shiny and sharply pointed. Sumac sounds Mesoamerican, but in fact comes from the Arabic *summaq*, meaning red. As we walk the road in spring, the young sumac flowers, arrowhead-shaped and fist-sized, stand out with their chartreuse tone, the brilliant green of new life. When fall comes around, the seeds have dried to a deep red, soon to be followed by the vibrant red-orange of the surrounding leaves. Since they present at eye level, they gain a little prominence against the gold background of popple, birch, and maple. They stand out, saying it's time to change our thinking, move away from the comfort of warm days and into the brisk evenings of the season to come.

The sumac is sheltered by the young white pine standing just a few feet to the west. It helps keep the winds from bending the sumac, perhaps helps it hold a little more moisture. Our sumac is isolated by the road but has relatives growing up on the neighbor's place across the blacktop. It is an outlier and, as such, subject to more risk. More than once I've come closer than I wished with the lawnmower or snowblower. It's at the northern and western edge of its range here, though others of its genus grow in the West.

As an edge plant, it has a hardiness that permits it to move in where spaces open up, so I hope our sumac stays for the long haul. There are bigger and bolder trees, but I feel a twinge of pride to know my own sumac stands here, a reminder every day that it's good to be a kid, if just in memory.

Probing

North American Deer Mouse
Peromyscus maniculatus

There was a time when I lived alone in my grandfather's cabin in the Harrison Hills for a few months. I was working on a big project, something that had grabbed my attention almost unexpectedly. The vision I was making real would shape my life for the next seven years. In the days I would sit by the window at my manual Smith-Corona and type, trying to turn a notion into words, plans, and applications. When stuck for words, which happened often, I'd get up, circle the small interior, step out the door, and walk along the drive under the hemlocks until my head cleared and the words would come again.

It was fall and evening came early. After my walk down the road to the small lake, my simple dinner, and the fading of light, I'd sit by the window and read. Then would come faint scratching somewhere by the kitchen counter. The mice were at it again.

By watching closely, soon I learned where they appeared, popping up through a crevice next to a supporting post that ran through the counter. Through trial and error, I came up with a live trapping system. It involved an empty mayonnaise jar and an apple. The apple went in the jar, toward the bottom, and the jar was carefully placed on its side by the crevice. Then I would listen for the scratching. When the sound changed to the scrabble of tiny paws on glass, it was my cue to leap from my chair, cross the room in two steps, and quickly turn the jar mouth against the backsplash. I missed the first couple of times, but soon I had it down and was a skilled live trapper of mice.

I would quickly turn the jar up and screw on an airhole-punched lid. Then I could look over my captive. The mice were lively, brownish-gray critters, bristling with whiskers, two-toned with a soft white on the belly, underlegs, and tail. Their name, deer mouse, comes from their jumping ability, something I knew all about from times when I wasn't quick enough with the jar lid. They are not close relatives of the scuttling house mice; both are in the order Rodentia, but they belong to different families. With their brown backs and white bellies, they seemed more to be woods animals akin to the chipmunk, clean with outdoor living and well attuned to what was going on around them. I turned more than a dozen loose again in the forest, in a place down the driveway and across the paved road. I read years later that they rarely migrate more than five hundred feet, so my one-thousand-foot hike to the release point was probably a safe distance to prevent their return. I could have plugged the hole where they entered the cabin, but that would have spoiled the fun.

When we built our new home by the lake, many years

later, the most prominent appearance of the deer mouse was right at the start, during the construction. We returned from a family visit to find the contractors had poured the concrete basement walls and floor. Inside the open basement, a deer mouse crouched in the corner, captive in a new, alien world of gray pavement.

We found a ladder and climbed down in to see how the mouse was. My trapping experience taught me they're prone to dehydration and can expire in a few hours without water. This mouse seemed a bit groggy. Todd and Eric, ages three and six, hunkered down by the mouse, looking it over thoroughly. It would move a few inches, but no more. Its beady eyes were trained on us, no doubt wondering what we would do next.

We looked around the construction site and found a spare cardboard box. The mouse didn't object to being nudged into the box with a chunk of 2x4, nor did it try jumping out on the trip up the ladder. At the edge of the woods, it crawled listlessly under the layer of dead leaves, in a damp area where we hoped it found the moisture it needed.

Perhaps it wasn't such a good favor to do. In years to come, the deer mice—no doubt, descendants of the one we rescued—would find ways under the garage door and up among the roof trusses. After midnight they were scratching about up there, rummaging through the insulation in vain hope of some nourishment. We did some enclosure work and sealing to make sure, for the time being at least, they would stay in their outdoors so we could sleep more peacefully indoors. The deer mouse is one of those creatures that lets you know you are living in their forest. Your efforts to control your space don't really have a chance when put up against their persistent hunger and curiosity.

Growing

Aspen
Populus tremuloides, Quaking
Populus grandidentata, Bigtooth

Popple, red maple, and northern red oak dominate the small piece of forest we own. Together they make a story of forest succession, of trees taking back open spaces and rebuilding a forest first the popple, then the true hardwoods. They tell the history of our place as a former farm field. Farming ended in the early 1960s. The popples are mature now, some of them big trees of twelve inches or more in diameter. True to their nature, they're starting to die out, making more room for the emerging maple and oak.

Both kinds of common aspen, quaking and bigtooth, are in our woods. A lone quaking aspen stands near the southeast corner, not far from the intersection of lake and bog. Its lower reaches are gnarly gray, but above it flashes the bright white bark that sometimes causes confusion with its distant cousin, the birch. The quaking aspen mentions to us that, out in Colorado and such, it's the lovely aspen of the mountains, the golden tree of fall. Here it's just popple, the weed tree of northern Wisconsin. They shoot up fast, break easily, are quickly taken down by the feller-buncher and taken to the pulp mill. But this is mostly bigtooth country. Their olive-tinted trunks surround the house. Their bigger and more jagged leaves collect in sharp-scented piles in the autumn yard.

The first task of living here was to saw down a cluster of bigtooth where the house now stands. Dressed in my lumberjack shirt, jeans, and "bungalow" boots, with my father's loaned chainsaw in hand, I felled, bucked, and limbed. After a couple of hours, though, one of the bulkier trees got the best of my rusty sawyer technique. The saw pinched and stayed pinched; no amount of wiggling would retract it, and the heavy tree could not be budged. I had no wedges, nor any way to fashion one. A partly sawed tree is a dangerous thing; a tree with a saw stuck in it is a damned thing. After some grumpy thoughts about my dilemma, I drove to the nearby small engine dealer, where I sheepishly asked to rent a saw. The owner just grinned, saying, "Here, borrow this one." Careful wood surgery followed, trimming the juicy wood near the bound blade, until I was able to drop the tree and give the tool its freedom again.

The popple announce their presence most loudly through their reproductive habits. Catkin season comes toward the end of spring. The yard suddenly has a blanket of fuzz, with embedded strings of brown and green seeds. The fuzz will wash away soon, but where the seeds have landed, a line of tiny plants will be grasping for a toehold.

Popple shoots, the stealth cloning network of the trees, invade the lawn all summer long. They push up from long roots underneath, putting on a practical demonstration of how the aspen feel about open spaces. Mowing them off discourages them, but they always lurk there, hoping the mower will go on hiatus and allow them to do their job of founding a new tree.

The popple come first, but they cannot stay. They've evolved for a limited lifespan, then get shaded out or replaced by the sturdier, shade-resistant hardwoods and pines. They shed blackened, dead limbs readily. Branches rattle down on the deck when stiff winds come, or drop suddenly into the yard.

In breezy conditions, the most common fate of the popple may take hold. A thud and a tangle of branches means one of them has lost its top. The tree snaps off twenty or thirty feet above the ground. There's been no visible weak spot there, but now the stub shows a blackened heart. Things have been rotting within.

The property came with a truly massive popple. When we cleared the yard, at its edge on the east stood a thick trunk at least three feet in diameter. It had the look of the sinister tree in the "Ferngully" movie, one of Todd's favorites. The prevailing winds pointed away from the yard and my garden, but I knew this one had the slow heartwood decay. It was too big for me to handle. It would have to come down wherever and whenever wind and gravity chose.

I needn't have worried. True to type, the top went first, collapsing one day in a northerly direction and just missing the lawnmower shed. The bulky snag then became a favorite of the pileated woodpeckers. They punched fist-sized slivery holes into the body, weakening it further, until one day the trunk fell into the woods. Afterward I could look out the window and see only a chunk of the formerly threatening tree, bark long peeled away, a hollow shell of punky gray stuff. Also in view: its neighbor to the north, getting pretty big and ready to take its place as the large, threatening presence over the yard.

Weed tree, pioneer tree, unloved tree—the popple is one more thing: the most commercially desirable forest product of northern Wisconsin. Its soft interior converts well to pulp, then becomes newsprint or similar papers of general use. "Peeling pulp" was a way for my high school friends to make some extra dollars for expenses like gas and prom tickets. You worked with a spud, a kind of long handled metal bar, to shell the loosely coupled bark off the eight- foot logs. Stacks of peeled popple stand here and there along the gravel roads of our territory, waiting for snorting diesel trucks with gaunt rattly trailers to haul them away. They go to Park Falls or Duluth to become big rolls of newspaper, or to Phillips or Hayward to run through a chipper and be pressed into sheets of board, materials to sheathe new construction. Our house has some chipboard in the walls branded with the logo of the big Louisiana-Pacific Hayward plant. A hundred years ago, someone building a house here would have cut the trees at hand and made planks on the spot. Our home and shelter is the product of industrial processes and technologies, aided and abetted by very cheap power and transportation. Still, it gives some comfort to know our walls contain some popple that may have grown right down the road from here.

Surviving
Western Painted Turtle
Chrysemys picta bellii

Movement in the late June grass, on the lawn alongside the house. Todd walks over to find out what is visiting our yard. "Dad, it's a turtle." No surprise; it's egg-laying season, the crucial time for turtles to come out on land and do what they can to continue the species.

The painted turtle is a little larger than my hand when fingers are spread. It's marching with determination away from the lake, uphill. Though we would love to pick it up to admire its decorated underside, the plastron, we won't interfere with the important business of its day. We just follow and watch. The turtle speeds up a bit, perhaps concerned about its audience. It looks at us with what seems like a baleful eye, though in truth, most turtles give you a dirty look when you meet. They do not trust us. Todd and I and Eric, who has joined us, keep our distance, move back a bit.

In the next ten minutes, the march of the turtle takes it through the lawn, onto the gravel driveway, and out on the blacktop road. There is little traffic on our dead-end, but we stand guard on each side of this traveling reptile, just in case.

Safely across, this mama turtle finds, on the edge of our neighbor's gravel driveway, the conditions she seeks. It's sandy here, not too stony, and though she may not know it, safe from the tires that will pass a couple of feet away. She settles to the ground, begins to scrape with a hind foot. Soon she has both hind feet at work, burrowing backward into the soft dirt.

The turtle stays in her chosen spot for a couple of hours. The small, rubbery eggs must be coming out, but we can't see this. She is on top, sheltering and protecting the whole process. We go away for a while, and when we come back, the nest is cleanly covered up. The turtle is already gone, out of sight. Downhill in any direction will have taken her back to water. She might come back to make another nest next year, or never again. The embryos are on their own.

The embryos are on their own, with every scavenger of the forest hunting them, as they can only grow in their shells and wait for what happens. Foxes, skunks, raccoons, snakes, probably even crows, will dig up and savor the contents of a nest. I see dug-up nests along the roadside as I drive and wonder what percentage aren't raided. Sometimes it seems as if the only turtles that get to hatch are those whose eggs are somehow overlooked by over-eager raccoons during the excavation.

Those that hatch will still face these predators, and more. North of about the Illinois border, hatchlings stay in their nest overwinter, clustered together, waiting it out as they must do in every winter to come. After the thaw, each will set out on tiny legs for a long, long trek to the lake. Epic stories could be told, of obstacles, of narrow escapes, if the voice of the turtle could be heard. But at the end, tiny turtles will plunge into the waterways, sensing somehow that these are their natural homes, the places where they will find nurture, protection, and the sunlight they crave to warm their air-temperature bodies. They will survive, eat plants and water bugs, grow up and sun themselves on logs and rocks, wait out winter under the ice. They are of an ancient, ancient kind, and things have worked out for them here.

I learned as a kid to catch turtles, big and small, while poling a green plywood pram up and down a slow-moving reach of the Couderay River. One time I hit the hatch just right, finding the weed beds crammed with silver-dollar-sized mini turtles, both painted and snapping. Soon I had thirteen of them scratching about the bottom of the pram. They had a ride up the river; then were released back into the floating green mats of water plants.

Eric and I once met a medium-sized painted turtle in the center of Delta Lake on an Opening Day fishing trip. We had gotten up early, loaded the canoe and our fishing rods, and driven the half-hour over to the county park landing. We launched into a warming spring day with just a slight breeze, a few frayed clouds overhead in the brightening blue. We headed out on the lake to fish some weed bed edges. If you spend time on the water in turtle country, you'll begin to recognize a turtle snout coming up for air and know the difference in its motion from water-logged sticks and other flotsam. Unexpectedly, we came upon this voyaging turtle, the size of a small pie-plate. In water they move swiftly, diving and holding their breath for many minutes, counting on our impatience and their concealment. But this one was not quick on this day, and I scooped it in so we could see it better. I let it go in the canoe, where it scrambled for shelter under Eric's seat in the bow.

We paddled a few more strokes as the scrabbling continued. "Daddy, you can put it back in the lake now." I obliged, and we were all happier for it.

In our territory the western painted turtle is by far the common kind, with its dark green carapace, racy striped yellow-and-green neck and legs, and bright, artistic plastron. Softshell turtles are sometimes along the waterways of some area rivers that feed eventually into the Mississippi. They have platter-sized, gray-green shells and pointed noses, giving them a jaunty, streamlined look. On a trip down the Namekagon below Trego, Deb and I once watched dozens of softshells slide off their basking logs as we came into view.

Big snappers were also part of my early days, stumping their way up the banks of the Couderay to make nests at the roadside, hissing and offering a wicked beak to anyone and anything approaching. The color of muck, with pebbled hide on her legs like the river bottom, the snapping turtle would lay a huge clutch of eggs resembling ping-pong balls. At least once we dug up a few, took them in, and tried to fry them. We found the yolks would cook, but the whites remained soft, runny. We had to try a taste, and tasted, we thought, a fishy, muddy flavor, though that might have been in our imaginations.

Rarest of all is the wood turtle, known for its shell, whorled like a carven piece of hard maple. It likes spending its days on land, but not too far from water. Bottom lands, places where the stream overflows during the melt and drains away for summer, are their favored home. Back in college, my herpetology professor led us into the Chequamegon National Forest to a known habitat not far from a small river. We walked through the waist-high weeds among the green ash trees and, sure enough, the woodies were there. They lurked in high grasses and brush, keeping the slow-moving flow of the river in sight.

The turtle goes back about 170 million years, or about three times earlier than the arrival of us primates. It came in the Middle Jurassic, the time of massive water creatures: plesiosaurs, oversized crocodiles, other toothy swimmers. The turtle's armor might have evolved as a way of avoiding the role of lunch for these hungry reptile cousins. It continues to serve, in maturity warding off all but the most desperate opponents, who, after all efforts, find little to munch on inside the bony casing. We sometimes kill them, run them over, pollute or destroy the places they live. But they move ahead, quite independent of us. They have a long future before them, whether or not we are part of it.

Falling

Northern Red Oak
Quercus rubra

It's a soul-stopping thing to suddenly wake in the night to loud, unexpected noise. This sound began with a low crackling, then advanced to crunching, tearing, and snapping. Long, long before the end, sleep-fogged as I was, I knew a massive tree was on its way down. I had time to hope the next sounds would not be the ricocheting thud and crunch against the building, the crash of glass. A few quick moments and the thump came, but on the ground, not the house. Catch the breath and let the heart go back where it belongs.

Explorations by flashlight, out the bathroom window, showed a green tangle on the southeast side, down by the bog. In the daylight, we found the largest trunk in a spreading cluster of oak had simply tipped over, laying out to the north. We'd had rains lately. The wet roots could no longer support the body, weakened by rot in the crotch near the base, so down she came at three a.m.

There'd been a preview of sorts a few years earlier. We all arrived home together from work and day care on an early summer day. Walking past the northeast bathroom door, I stopped, wondering why no light was coming in the window. A solid mass of leaves pressed against it. We trotted outside and found a small oak, growing thirty-some feet from the wall, had come down, its top neatly resting against the side of the house. A few feet shorter and it would have missed; a few feet taller and it would have whomped down on the roof. A branch had put a long scratch in the siding, but otherwise we were undamaged. I walked down the road and borrowed a neighbor's chainsaw, along the way attracting a following of neighborhood kids. Eric, Todd, and their friends observed as I cut away the limbs and dragged the hunks of wood into the brush, building a pile that would soon harbor some of our scurrying woods neighbors.

A couple of oaks stand in the front yard along with two red maples. When we built here, they were slim poles, shoots coming up under the popple overstory. I saved them to shade the yard. They were beaten up on occasion by departing construction trucks, but they survived and have since put on substantial wood. When fall comes around, they give a contrast to the flaming statements of the maples, their red a more muted, somber tone. Oak leaves by the mound, smelling sharply of their tannin, stack up in the yard. The fall rains make them soggy, but we wait for a dry day. Then we sweep the piles into the woods, shoving them so they aren't pushed back into the yard by the early winter winds.

The other product of the oak, the acorn, is very much prized here. The black and gray squirrels dive about, toting them off to their secret spots. Acorn time is a well-defined point in fall, when pops and rattles echo as the nuts bounce off the deck like popcorn kernels.

Red oak is a tree of value in human enterprise, a reliable citizen and contributor to our homes and buildings. Our oaks are near the northern edge of their range; they taper off just across the Canadian border as the boreal forest of spruce and birch takes over. Their best country is southward. I've walked among huge red oaks on Deb's family farm near Cadott, checking the branch sockets where squirrels and raccoons nest. From time to time the farm oaks are selectively harvested, put through a sawmill and turned into inch boards. We have some of that oak lumber in our house, forming sturdy door frames. The planks were nailed up through drilled holes; they were so rock solid you couldn't drive a spike into them. Our oak living room furniture was made in a small factory a few miles from the farm.

Farther still to the south, the prairie oak forests of western Illinois sheltered my forebears when they came to America. At the Red Oak Restaurant in Bishop Hill, Illinois, we've looked out at the Swedish Colony buildings, their posts and beams cut from the nearby timber, which still grows not far beyond. The people who built these big wooden structures came with little in their pockets but brought with them the skill to work the hard wood and make things of practical use. Our oaks remind us of those oft-forgotten skills, but we are happy just to have them here, bringing their enduring quality to these woods.

Multiplying

Common Merganser
Mergus merganser

Rain thrums on the roof, on a cold day of so-called spring. There is comfort in this, despite the bleary look of the outdoors. When it's your own roof that's keeping you dry, you can have a little feeling of establishment, of owning one thing solid and waterproof to protect you and yours. You are unimaginably better off than your nameless ancestor who sheltered in heaps of brush or under dodgy shelves of rock. Your family will be all right here.

Out on the water, small black shapes are cruising about. They're buffleheads, little ducks with round black bodies and a bright spot of white at the back of the head. Their home is saltwater in the winter and far northern shores in nesting season. They're up from the Gulf or the Carolinas, and their destination might be the Arctic Ocean. Do they carry a memory of our small lake as a favored stopover, or is it just one of hundreds of possible pitstops around here? We'll never know. Here they are, and here they rest a few hours before the next push north.

Mallards will also come through, and occasionally a woodie. We don't see the "bluebills", the greater and lesser scaup that passed through here in great flights ninety years ago. These flocks drew the hunting and writing attention of Gordon MacQuarrie, the great outdoor writer who roamed our territory. Their numbers are smaller now, and this may not be a place that suits them.

If a duck is to pause longer here, check the scenery and the menu, and choose to nest, it will be a common merganser. Even this is a rarity; we usually have no resident ducks. But now and then a year comes when a merganser pair makes a home here.

The availability of fish probably factors strongly into the year-to-year value of our lake as a merganser nesting habitat. Like their far-distant dinosaur forebears, ducks come in two types: plant eaters and meat eaters. Most of the familiar ducks are vegetarians, savoring various kinds of slimy pondweeds, plus delicacies such as wild rice. Mergansers, with their saw-toothed beaks, have evolved to chase fish.

The mergansers themselves offer nothing like the gaudy paint jobs of the wood duck or the harlequin duck, nor the sharp color accents of the mallard or the teal. Yet they are handsome birds, each sex in its own way. The males, at a glance, can be mistaken for loons, having black backs and heads, trimmed with white below. Females are a mottled gray, with a burnt orange head sporting a jagged punk-rock hairdo behind. Both have orange beaks; this is the easiest way to distinguish the male from a loon, which will always have a black bill.

When the season arrives, mama mergansers are trailed in the water by a long string of bobbing puffball ducklings. They're already ducking to grab small minnows or tasty bugs out of the brine of the nearby lily pads. Another attraction of this lake is that there are no torpedoing northerns or muskies concealed under those pads. When the bass get big, however, a mother must keep a close eye on her train, lest there be a splash and a sudden disappearance.

When the mergansers are there, we sit on our bench on the shore and watch the parades. The ducklings grow so quickly. In a matter of a few weeks, they will be practicing flights around the circle of water. Then we'll see them fly together in formation, building up strength. And one day they're not here anymore.

Watching the mergansers suggests to us that we could make more effort to be efficient and leave no trace. They come, nest in a low-key way, quickly raise their families, and then move on. If fortunate, they attract little attention. They don't even make much noise.

We tell ourselves we'll try to do better. At the very least, we'll take the time to enjoy where we are as fully as we are able. We'll step away more often from the distractions of modern life, the shallow things that so easily capture our attention. As the living things around us grow and change, we can take note and enjoy what we learn from them. We can start, at least, by making sure we count the merganser ducklings when they're here, when they paddle through the lily pads and out into the open water.

ROAMING

Eastern Timber Wolf
Canis lupus lycaon

In my younger days, in the county to the southeast, the timber wolf was just a rumor. Traps and swift shots had brought them down for the bounty the state paid on the remains of a threatening carnivore. Coyotes snuck about, hanging out up by the town dump, but quickly sliding back into the brush when you came into their view. They had learned to expect hot lead. They were wild and canine, but we knew they weren't wolves. A wolf would have had a different attitude.

A neighbor who spent time in the woods knew a little more. There was a big section of wild land a few miles off to the west. "There's wolfs in there. I seen them, for sure. They don't come out much, and they run quick." He figured he would get one someday, even though the state had dropped the bounty when it decided there were no wolves left. What he would do with it, hard to say. It was just what you did, when you had the gun in your hand and the wolf came in sight.

The wolf came back on its own. Maybe that phantom pack off to the west started it, it and others like it spreading out after so many years laying low. Just as probable, it wandered in from Minnesota, young wolves roaming eastward to find new territories empty of rival packs. The game managers learned it was there, began keeping track. And eventually the wolf became well-known again, and everyone had an opinion on it.

There was no question the wolf would bring down vulnerable livestock when it could, whether wild deer or young cattle. And there was no question *ma'ingan* holds a strong, spiritual role in the story of the Anishinaabe, that in their dream history it belongs here. The fact that it contributes to the land community can be shown. The fact that it has few enemies here, save its own kind, its diseases, and humanity, is the hard part of the puzzle.

The state pays for the cattle while the farmers are unhappy about the unpredictable losses and the trouble. The hunters grumble about the deer kills, even though these are almost always the weak and sick. The wildlife advocates and Native people speak up in favor of letting the wolf live. Members of Congress push and tug out East, each with their own idea of what the wolf is, what it means, what it might and might not do in days to come, what might be done to it.

Back home, the wolf is here, and it will stay around. Better than any of us, it knows where the back forty is, where the tracks of hunters fill with snow after the deer hunt ends. It likes this country, and, with its long, lanky legs, it will roam much of it. There is sandy earth for digging dens and enough space to bring out the pups for learning and growing.

I've seen the wolf just once near our place on the little lake. Driving home one late afternoon, a mile from the driveway, I saw a big canine flash across the blacktop a few yards ahead. It was dark, grayish, not the yellow-brown of *el coyote,* and far too large. The wolf was running full tilt, directly toward our house. Though my children were probably out in the yard, I knew it was no threat. After its dash to cross the road, it would lie in the bushes for a short rest. Then it would slip off through the nearby swamp or pass along the ridge to the south of the lake, staying away from the houses and bright lights. The wolf was just another part of this place where we had chosen to live.

GLIDING

Eastern Garter Snake

Thamnopis sirtalis sirtalis

Snakes naturally make many people uncomfortable. Their legless motion, swift and sinuous, is alien to us bipeds and quadrupeds. Snakes appear unexpectedly and vanish quickly into nooks and tunnels we cannot explore. And some of them have reputations of venom and attitude.

There are no poisonous snakes north of Wisconsin's midsection, a dividing line usually identified by State Highway 29. Even in the southern part of the state, the rattlesnakes of the Coulee region and the big river valleys are rarely seen. They're shy, docile creatures, wanting nothing to do with people and everything to do with little creeping rodents in the grasses and thickets. And the same can be said for the snakes in our neighborhood.

The best snake to find is the red-bellied, or fire, snake. These little reptiles are too small to have much of a bite to worry about, and they rarely even try to use it. They are a handsome cordovan color on top, with a secret below: the bright glow of a scarlet belly. Far too small to eat a vole or mouse, they hunt bugs through the weeds and the dried remnants of the past season's tree cover. Eric and Todd have learned to hold the snake gently, just behind the head. But better to just watch it as it squirms its way through the edge territory between lawn and forest.

The grass snake is a similar size and equally beautiful in its chartreuse scales. It too is a calm, quiet animal, happy to be left alone. When disturbed, it swiftly fades back into the green stems around it.

The grass snake and fire snake are rarities here, but you have a good chance of coming across a garter snake. They find sunlit logs down by the lake, or sometimes in the woods, to sun and get their blood moving. Their black-and-yellow striping is good camouflage, so they can be startling when seen, given away by movement in an unexpected place. Some grow to two feet or more.

The largest of our reptiles is also the best hidden. The fox snake, commonly called "pine snake" here, can be more than three feet long, tan with dark brown, diamond-like markings. Those markings, and its habits of shaking its tail and striking when threatened, cause people to view it with distrust, as if it were a timber rattler in disguise. I have seen pine snakes intentionally run over, pelted with fist-sized rocks, and on one occasion picked up by an eager dog and shaken to death. They seem to be fewer in number now, or maybe they continue to learn to stay out of sight.

Pine snakes are known to climb large evergreens. That's probably how the snake my father met got into his house. He loved to read and owned many books, one of which he wanted on a warm summer day. The book was in a narrow storage space upstairs. The only access involved crawling on hands and knees through a tunnel-like place under the eaves. Flashlight in hand, he crawled in to find before him...the snake. He was a brave man and made a grab for it, but it slid away under a loose floorboard. That house was nearly a hundred years old, with its share of snake-sized crevices. Our house here is new and tight. So I tell myself. But I keep an eye out for pine snakes. I'd rather meet one on my own terms.

Pine snakes and grass snakes are egg layers, hiding their nests in rotting logs or abandoned rodent burrows. I imagine mice might exact a kind of vengeance by making a lunch of any snake eggs they come across. Garters and red-bellied snakes have a solution. They are ovoviparious—that is, they produce eggs but keep them in their bodies, delivering the young when they break out of their shells, still inside.

As I look out in spring across our small woods, it stretches the imagination to picture clutches of snake eggs, with tiny snakelets worming their way into the world and starting to roam about. And that's just a tiny part of the actions of nature right there, to be seen if we can be still, listen, and look closely at everything before us.

Communing

Eastern Chipmunk
Tamias striatus

A secret city hides right in front of the deck. A few of its concealed gates are known. One is just below the bird feeder, strategically placed for access to black sunflower seeds dropped off the hanging bin. Another, just inside the woods line, gives access to good cover, including hazelnuts and juneberries growing nearby. No doubt there are more hidden openings about, ways to quickly get in and out of the network of tunnels and cavities below. Chipmunks never do anything that is not done quickly.

The chipmunk and the black-capped chickadee are the most common of animals in our northern highland forest. When I see one of these, I know I'm home. If it's a time of year when the ground is bare but the feeders are out, both species are going to be active outside the windows. The chipmunks dart out of the sheltered burrows, pack the cheeks, and are gone. They are not too shy to climb up and high-walk the deck railing, scanning the earth below for scattered seeds that have been knocked down by the birds. The chickadees, meanwhile, do their complex territorial dance to and from the feeder. Each bird is aggressive enough to get a shot at clinging to the wire to peck out the tasty sunflower hearts, but it can hold turf for only a moment. Its fellows are already flying at the perch, chasing it away for their turn.

For pure entertainment value, though, none of these can beat the gray squirrels, most of which here have black fur. Their lives are spent scooting up and down the oaks, nesting in high cavities where limbs have broken off and rotted away. Their aerial acts from limb to limb catch the breath. Only the slimmest bit of springy branch, across feet of space, is there to save them from a very long fall. Yet I've never seen a squirrel drop.

The battle of the bird feeders outside our windows went on for well over a decade. We hung them from hooks, from wires. We bought squirrel baffles and roofed feeders. Nothing dismayed the persistent rodents. They could walk yards out on the horizontal wire and just as quickly scramble back, suspended by claws. If they reached the hanging feeder, they draped over the baffle, back toes clinched around the suspending hook, and munched away from the feeder tray below.

It took a long, long time, but one day we realized a bird feeder will always also be a squirrel feeder. Once the squirrels had their fill, the birds could get theirs. We bought more bulging bags of sunflower seeds and resigned ourselves to more regular refills.

In the early spring, snow still on the ground, the squirrels chase each other in pairs across the lawn and up the nearest oak. It's a sure sign there will be young squirrels in the near future. An early chipmunk is nearby, working the seeds below the feeder. It pops up on the deck, ascends the rail, then sits there and scratches itself like a dog. Another sharp movement and it's gone, down into the tunnels in the yard below our feet, into the lodgings where its family of tiny munklets may be growing. There the chipmunk engineers have dealt with important technical problems: routing around rocks, dealing with moisture and drainage, managing space and the growth of families, handling supply and security. Such worlds we do not and cannot know.

FLOCKING

Evening Grosbeak
Coccothraustes vespertinus

It's the first few days of winter. We're excited because a bird we have not seen is here. It's a larger version of a goldfinch, with similar blunt beak and eye-catching black, white, and bright yellow trim. The head is black, giving a kind of hooded look. It perches at our feeder, and soon there is another like it. The Audubon guide tells us these are evening grosbeaks.

Throughout this winter, three or four grosbeaks become regular customers. They include a female, trimmed the same but with pale gray in place of the gold. The birds are robin-sized. In most ways they're like a differently-colored edition of the rose-breasted grosbeak, which also has been here, though rarely. We are in the middle of the summer range for the rose-breasted with its bright bib, white belly, and black back. But when these head for Central America in the fall, their yellow-backed boreal relations may come down from Canada to spend the cold months here, right on the boundary between their summer and winter ranges.

Goldfinches are a more common visitor. They are here

in the shoulder seasons and occasionally in summer. Half a dozen will mob the feeder, blocking out the usually aggressive chickadees. They push each other, shouldering their way in. When there is a finch at every perch, the feeder is a gaudy Chinese lantern, dangling and swaying as it displays bright, flashing decoration.

For their size, the evening grosbeaks also have a lot of energy at the feeder. Munching sunflower seeds with their chunky beaks, they jump about, fluttering wings for balance. We wonder where these big birds spend the rest of their chilly days. Probably they tuck into a balsam or other conifer nearby, gaining shelter from energy-sapping breezes. Our neighbors tell us the small flock makes the rounds every day, hitting each feeder along the road with regularity and vigor. Perhaps they range even farther, over the hill to the big lake where yet more feeders are filled to their liking.

Even more grosbeaks appear the following winter. They are with us for another year or two. Then, one day, we realize we haven't seen them for a few winters. They do not return.

Migration is not mandatory for these birds. If there are food and shelter for them up in the Canadian wilderness, they stay put. Like the redpolls, grosbeaks come south when their food supply gets slim. Maple seeds are their favorite natural snack, so there must have been several years of poor seed production north of us. Now the maples must be back on track, and the birds are staying on their range.

Memories of the grosbeaks linger with us. Their slightly clownish appearance was a welcome entertainment outside our windows. Once in a while, when a goldfinch is at the feeder, we think of their larger relatives and dream of a bright winter day when they will come back to visit.

Penetrating

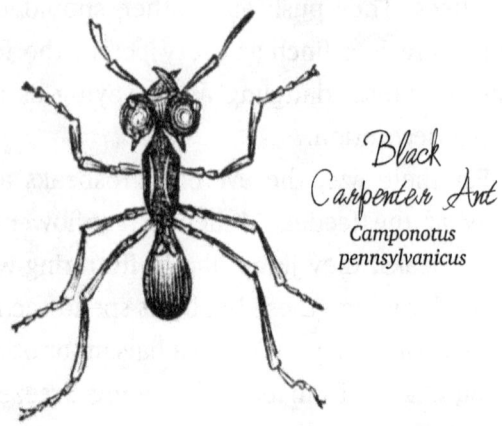

Black Carpenter Ant
Camponotus
pennsylvanicus

You think of your new house as a closed, impenetrable box. You're in control: what you want stays in; what you don't want is sealed out.

It's an environment you have defined, completely under your management. Nature didn't make it; you did.

Nature has an entirely different view of your house. It's just another part of the landscape. It's made of wood; it surrounds space and air. It contains heat, light, nutrients. As these assets are vital to your personal economy, so are they figured into the economy of what surrounds you. They're harder to put to use than the acorns, tadpoles, sunlight, or mushrooms, but they are known to be present, and they have their place in the balance sheet of what's available. You might think your things are tightly locked up, but there are always narrow cracks and tiny gaps. Something tiny will assuredly find them.

It was a few years before the first ant was sighted. It poked along the baseboard, roaming over the living room carpet. It had wandered out of the bushes and into lunar territory. It was noticed, but not squashed. It was medium-sized and dark-colored, not possible to ignore. But it might be lost and would surely disappear. It did.

Then there were a few more. After a while, it was not a rare thing to see an ant. Then, one day, they appeared inside the dishwasher. Giving them a nice hot run through the wash cycle should have discouraged them. It didn't.

I noticed a few grains of sawdust on the basement floor, in a place where I hadn't been sawing. I tipped the ceiling tile above; scrambling black ants and glistening white ant eggs spilled out. We had a carpenter ant problem, all right.

I knew this was beyond my skills to solve. I needed a jack of all trades. Asking around the neighborhood, I was pointed to a guy named Marv. He came over to check out the ant situation.

Marv probed with a screwdriver at the outside frame of the door to the deck, directly above where I'd found the ants and eggs. "Here, you've got rot setting in. Ants love wet wood. They're coming in here. It's rotting because your deck is built too high." I had built the deck myself. It was another lesson in how much I didn't know. "The deck channels the water into the doorframe. We'll need to lower it and replace the frame."

We ordered a replacement doorframe. Marv and his crew came and sawed, jacked, blocked, and leveled. One rung was trimmed off the short steps leading to the lawn. When finished, the deck was just as it had been, but six inches lower. Then, on a warm day, Marv came back, ripped out the doorframe, then cut out the punky sill. He asked to borrow our shop vac. "I gotta suck a lot of ants out of there." And so the ants went.

A few years later, suddenly there were teensy ants around the kitchen sink. I traced a marching line back to the windowsill above the sink. On the outside wall, the line came up from the foundation, over the siding, then disappeared into the window frame. There didn't seem to be rot; these ants had just found a way in, a way to something they liked. Some work with caulk and tools plugged the crack, ending the parade of the determined little army.

Plenty of ants are still making their lives around us. Their colonies are around the driveway. They like a sandy spot on the border of yard and woods. They're busy with good work: chewing up organic matter, helping dead wood decay, farming aphids, and tangling with other insects in the jungle of grass stalks.

A dead tree or stump with a mass of sawdust spilling out is a sure clue that ants are on task. They don't eat the wood, just chew tunnels through it, just as they did with the water-soaked sill below our deck door.

As for ant predators, we know one for certain: the black bear. On a family trip into the Boundary Waters Canoe Area Wilderness, not far north in Minnesota, Eric spotted a furry black shape near our campsite. The bear was tearing apart a rotted pine stump and slurping the resident ants out of their nest. The ants must have been biting back, but the bear didn't show it. Soon the bear would wander over for a look around our campsite for more substantial fare. But for the moment, we were grateful for those ants.

BLAZING

When June passes its midpoint, I am always watching a certain spot along the county highway as I make my daily drive to work. It's a little pocket marsh, next to a small house and right across from the intersection of two roads. Cattails are the long-term tenants here, but, as midsummer marches closer, a light blue tinge appears. Growing stronger day by day, the color brings to mind the intense flame of a propane torch, bright and volatile in blue violet, pale yellow at its throat. By the time the last day of June is coming into view, the wild irises own the marsh, flooding it with their bold energy.

Northern Blue Flag
Iris versicolor

This marsh brings memories of other northern places where the blue flag holds sway in June. A bigger marsh on the state highway leading south to Hayward, a wet swamp dotted with thick violet blobs, scattered around the dead spears of spruce rampikes. A place on the Thousand Island Lake Road by the Sylvania Wilderness of upper Michigan, where a moment's glance down an embankment brought a view of such intense blue, I had to look again. A clump of floating bog on a Sylvania lake nearby, iris stalks poking out at jaunty angles, each holding its brilliant bloom up as if to say, "Here, see this!"

Out in front of our house, at the water's edge, *versicolor* has but a minor toehold. The crisp green shoots come up in a few places among the shoreline grasses. They don't blossom every year, but when I see the pocket swamp blazing in June, I walk down by the water at home and sometimes find one or two nodding toward the lake.

The irises are pioneers here. They know the future of a shallow lake is a swamp, and they will help make it so. The weeds grow thicker, the dead leaves pile up in the lake bottom squish, the water lilies inch farther out toward the center. The iris roots push determinedly forward under the saturated soil. It might take three or four hundred years, but someday this lake will look a lot like the tiny marsh on the highway.

Take a look down the throat, and you'll see some of what the iris brings to the wetland. There are bugs living in there: tiny flies, maybe bigger spiders, all sorts of fauna. Out of sight are the rhizomes, contributing to the nourishment of the mucky soil below, helping hold bogs and shoreline marshes together, stretching out to make new clumps.

An Anishinaabe word found here and there on the northern Wisconsin map is *pacwawong*, or perhaps originally *pucwagawong*. It belongs to places where the water plants are thick along the shore, such as the wide water lake on the Namekagon above Seeley, and the drowned place in the Chippewa Flowage where a village once stood on the banks of a winding, marshy river. A number of meanings of *pacwawong* have been described over the hundreds of years Europeans have been trying to grasp the subtleties of the original language of this land. The one I love is "land of reed and flag." It seems to enfold in it the sweep of open waters, the movement of the breeze across the shore plants, the strong green smell of the marsh, and the calls of the redwings perched on the swaying stems. Pacwawong is a good place to canoe, to move with a swing and glide across the rippled surface, following the shoreline in the sun and wind. Here the *nabagashkoon* grow, their blue brushes echoing the color of water and sky at the height of the season of *niibin*, the best time of the year.

AMUSING

Raccoon
Procyon lotor

Working in the yard on a bright August afternoon, I suddenly heard a squalling sound. It repeated from somewhere close by in the woods. Eric came around the corner of the house and asked me what was making that noise.

We tracked the source to one of the big popples behind the lawnmower shed, between the house and the road. A few years back, hairy woodpeckers had bored a nest hole twenty feet up the trunk. I would hear the persistent calls of the woodpecker nestlings whenever I went to the shed. Now a different bulletin was being issued from the hole, which I could see had been enlarged. A small raccoon was peering out of the nest. Its muzzle opened and closed as it sent repeated shrill barks across the woods.

It didn't take long to learn more about what all the fuss was for. Eric heard rustling in the brush behind us. Soon an adult raccoon poked its nose from the nearby ferns. We moved off a short distance and watched the show. The parent waddled to the base of the tree, then scrambled rapidly up to the nest with surprising agility. Grasping the kit by the scruff with its mouth, it carefully backed down the tree, then marched back into the woods. We followed at a distance, watching as the big raccoon, still toting the now-quiet child, disappeared into the bog.

We guessed the noisy kit was the last of several being moved out of the nest. No doubt the growing family had exceeded available space in the former woodpecker nest. Mom (probably) was U-hauling them out into the bog, to a hollow log or a sheltered space in the thick wetland bushes. The last traveler to go was mighty upset about having been left by itself.

The biggest surprise was that they were there. Nesting surely had been going on for a couple of months, with plenty of attendant travel back and forth around the yard and through the trees close to the house. Yet this was the only time we noticed them, just as they closed business and headed on out.

Raccoons are rarely seen but always around. Their presence can be tested by forgetfully leaving a bin of garbage out overnight, if you don't mind cleaning up the mess the next day, and if the bear doesn't get there first. On occasion they've scrambled up the deck railing in the dark to reach for a hanging feeder. Caught when the deck lights pop suddenly on, they peer in at us from just a few feet outside the window, then bustle away. Their attitude shows caution but also a sense of ownership of the night. On warm evenings when we walk down the road in the dark, we can be startled by the skittering rattle of raccoon claws on the blacktop ahead of us.

It would be easy to picture them catching and washing food on the shore of the lake, but it lacks the freshwater clams and crawdads they love, so no piles of discarded shells or thorax chitin are to be found here. They must get by on plants, bugs, and what they can pick up around the homes in the neighborhood. Their omnivorous diet, corpulent gait, and intelligence cause folks to speculate they're closely related to bears. While there is a relationship, their nearest relatives are the canines.

In our part of the world, the most celebrated raccoon is Sterling North's Rascal. The book about the boy, his orphaned companion, and their adventures up and down the Brule River in a canoe built in the home parlor gives us a daydream of what we might find in the forest. In the end, Rascal had to go back to the wild, and that's where the raccoon belongs, as much as we tame them with easy food and appeals to their natural curiosity. While it's hard to say what their niche really is in our neighborhood ecology, it's certain the woods would be less entertaining without their masked presence.

DOMINATING

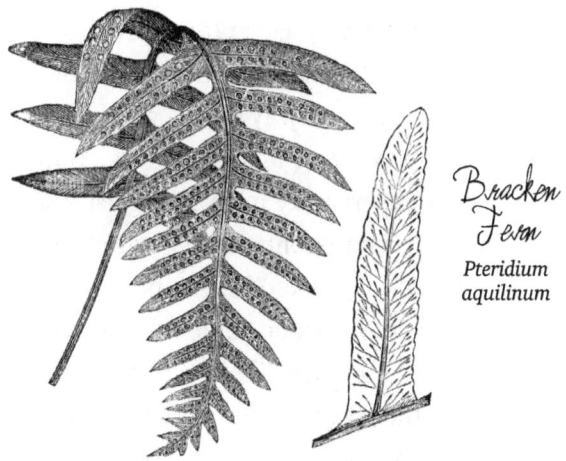

Bracken Fern
Pteridium aquilinum

The beaked hazel is the woody understory across our property. But where it does not claim the real estate, the bracken fern takes over. Ferns are as global as the wind, which takes their spores into many corners, cracks, and crannies where they can grab a toehold. Even on rocky ground, crevices usually hold a green frond or two. In our territory, they flow across the land, occupying any space where a little sunlight slips through and the soil gives up some moisture.

There are far more ferns than trees, but we notice them mainly in the spring, when the fiddleheads push up through the leaf litter. The curlicues, shaped like nothing else in the woods, catch the eye as they unfurl and fan out into the broad fronds. The name *aquilinium* comes from aquila, the Greek for "eagle", describing their wing-like shape.

Ferns have full claim on a few feet of the ditch between our driveway and the sumacs. There is an eye-pleasing mix of them:

brackens, sensitive ferns with their broader leaves, a few taller interrupted ferns. In this small place, the usually disheveled shapes of natural growth are replaced by something that's almost orderly, something close to a model for a fern garden one might create with spade and trowel. When I remember to look here, I always come away with a good feeling about what I see. I'm reminded of long-ago visits to the Sunken Garden in the Como Park Conservatory in St. Paul, just a short walk from the home of my grandparents. Ferns and moss sprouted from walls of moist, mossy stacked limestone crowding the narrow, winding pathway. And I wonder: do we like "gardens" because we create them, or do we like them because they speak of things we see in the larger world? The fern garden in our ditch was created only by random spores, but I love it.

Lacking any kind of blossom, ferns are the background, the anonymous greenery surrounding more prominent, brassy plants. It's the same role they play in a florist's arrangement. They provide shade for low-growing flowering plants that might otherwise dry out in the sun. When you enjoy seeing trilliums or harebells, take note of the modest green wings above that make them possible.

Bracken contains compounds that can make hooved animals ill, so the deer leave it alone. If eaten by insects, it can induce uncontrolled molting, a truly nasty trick, exhausting bugs to death. One of its compounds, ptaquiloside, is a known human and animal carcinogen, but it can be denatured through boiling. We've enjoyed cooked fiddleheads as a spring side dish; they have a mild vegetable flavor, a little like asparagus.

The scent of crushed ferns sticks in the memory. Walk through a patch, and the slightly acrid smell rises from what you've flattened underfoot. A lighter version of this odor is in the air on the hot days of July and August. It brings back a memory of pitching a tent on an overgrown campsite, the essence of mashed ferns mixing with old canvas and a whiff of woodsmoke.

When the weather turns cooler, the fern joins the deciduous leaves above in revealing its long-hidden tones. Briefly, there are waist-high fields of lemon and orange waves. Then all fades to a dull brown, the fronds shriveling until matted and crushed under the snowbanks. The bracken is fragile in all seasons, yet we never think twice about stepping on it or pushing it aside. Yet it is nothing if not persistent. It will be back soon, as it has been for millions of years.

Calling

Coyote
Canis latrans

The sky. The stars.

We run down the path to the ice-covered lake, darting forward in darkness. Out on our hand-shoveled ice rink, we slide and spin for a moment, then move closer together and gaze upward.

The entire universe is displayed before us. The whole thing. All we have to do is look.

I draw Todd close and point back, toward the house. "You see the Big Dipper?" I help him find the pointer stars that guide to Polaris. "If you can use the Dipper to find that star, you'll always know which way is north."

Turning back, we easily find brave Orion leaning upward in the southeast, his belt and sword glittering. At his knee, the white-hot young star Rigel; at his shoulder, ancient Betelgeuse, red-tinted beacon. Behind him, Sirius, brightest of all the stars, and lesser Procyon, his two roaming canines. Before him, plunging Taurus with his angry orange eye Aldebaran and the cluster of Hyades at the nose. There's a lot of action up there above us. Even more can be seen if we watch intently: cruising satellites, the flash of meteorites, the bright-white International Space Station sometimes crossing at its rock-steady pace above us. As we watch them, we wonder what they're seeing.

A few of our neighbors have yard lights, and we see the glow from the home windows, including our own. Out here, though, away from the shore, we look up and away from these intrusions, up and away into the deep blackness, into the ever-night of space around us.

Yet not an utter black. Our galactic lens swoops up toward Cassiopeia, the woman in the chair who sits opposite the Dipper. If we gaze at it long enough, we begin to see it as stars, stars beyond count, beyond comprehension. It can be unnerving at times. It can also be comforting. There's our home; that's the big place that surrounds where we live, the gently turning swirl that is our place on the map.

The sound begins off in the south, abruptly, interrupting our spacious thoughts. It's sharp, pitched high and biting, akin to the air around us and around it. It's raucous, gabbling, edgy. It resolves into yelps. "Coyotes," I say. Deb, Todd and Eric tilt their heads, hearing the distant calls. They must be three or four miles away, out in the wilder country that stretches below us.

Todd is puzzled. "What do you think they're doing?" We speculate that the pack might be letting others know they're present in their territory. Or they may have found something to eat, something worth sharing with their pack mates. One thing is certain: the wolves must not be nearby. When the wolf pack is running, the coyotes stay quiet. They know who's in charge, and that the wolves will take up their eons-long battle at any chance.

The calling goes on for just a few minutes. Then the quiet of January is back, the silence of a settled-down forest, full of life, but life that is waiting out the cold, ice, and snow for something better. We listen a few minutes more, thinking of those bright-eyed wild dogs, standing in an opening in the balsams and popples, heads turned up to this same sky, singing their ever-song, glad for the lives they have here, glad like us.

WADING

It's a wet spring. The lake is up, water pushed back into the bog laurel along the shoreline. In the bog below our home, just across the property line, a narrow horseshoe of water is open around the center cluster of plants and brush. As I look out the bathroom window, I glimpse movement back through the trees. There's something going about in the new channel.

Great Blue Heron
Ardea herodias

I slip down through the oaks and maples. Keeping my distance, I find I'm watching a pair of herons at work. The big birds move slowly, methodically, along the waterway, their sharp yellow eyes surveying the edges. Their spearheads of beaks are at the ready. Woe to any frog that makes an ill-advised stroke or hop when in range.

We've never seen a heron here before. They must have come in from a nesting place in the area, possibly over the hill to the west where a stream enters the big lake. The next day they are still there, or maybe they came back. Thinking of a musician, I nickname them Gil and Scott.

While their movements are usually quiet, occasionally

there is a splash from over that way. Was it lunch, or a miss? Gil and Scott are our neighbors for a few days. Then they spread their huge wings, launch from the bog, and do not return.

Heron rookeries are located where there are enough tall trees to support a colony, close to lakes or wetlands. On the Chippewa Flowage, a long, narrow island has long featured a campsite toward one end and a rookery toward the other. While camped there one year, we noticed the noise and activity and decided to quietly visit. We found the active nesting area using both sight and smell, via the large white splashes of fragrant bird droppings across the forest floor. Above, the ragged stick nests clustered near the treetops, almost concealed from our view. We couldn't see the herons, and we didn't think they saw us. But we could hear their murmuring and their movement noises up in the canopy. Below the nests, fragments of cracked shells and bones of unsuccessful nestlings littered the landscape.

There is something primitive and threatening about these huge, wild flyers, as though pterodactyls had returned from extinction. We slipped quietly back away through the woods, glad to not have a close-up meeting. More likely, if we had been detected, the adults would have flown.

During our stay at the campsite, herons cruised around us, sometimes low across the sweeping water of the flowage, other times high above, evoking storks as they flew with their characteristic tucked, S-curved necks and trailing legs. Watching the birds land is always entertaining. They swoop up on their chosen spot, spreading wide, then stall out and flap strongly for a soft setdown.

The nickname shypoke suits the heron well. They are indeed shy, never allowing even the quietest of paddlers to get too near, taking back to the air whenever a canoe comes in sight. And they do poke: walking slowly with their jerky gait into marshes and shorelands, probing with that bill, striking in a flash at the next target for their appetite. In their shyness and pokiness, they have an act that is theirs alone, largest of our waterbirds, and always exciting to see, in the water or on the wing.

Marching

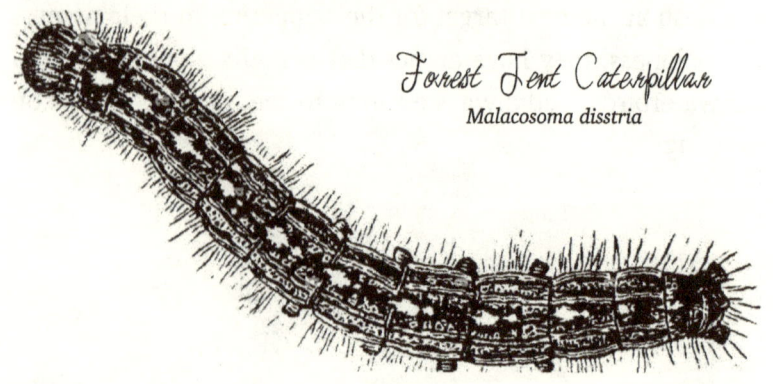

Forest Tent Caterpillar
Malacosoma disstria

It's on the house siding, crawling up. A narrow greenish-gray caterpillar with sporty medium-blue flanks, some orange accents, a row of white spots down the black back, and a bulbous head. Maybe two inches long. Such a little thing; such a big change it will bring. While a few forest tent caterpillars can be around any summer, we're overdue for an outbreak.

As I look at the creeper on its determined upward path, I remember a day in the past when I drove U.S. 2 west into Minnesota, near the St. Louis River bridge. Suddenly the surface of the highway seemed to begin moving in front of me, somehow flowing from north to south. Millions of "army worms" were on the march, hunting the next popple to denude. It almost made me dizzy to look. I slowed down, knowing the road could be slick as ice, as traffic squashed the masses of caterpillars into the blacktop. For miles, the worms were there, humping along heedlessly, pushed by their powerful appetite for leaves.

The summer brings more worms and some frayed-looking trees around the yard, but this is just the first foray. The following spring, the battalions emerge and go relentlessly to their task. All the fresh young aspen leaves are quickly gone; same for the birches. Even the oaks give up their new foliage. Only the red maples in and around the yard are not stripped; they give off chemicals the worms don't like. But even they look gnawed at the edges.

Trees and bushes are festooned with worms dangling like pendants from sticky silk strings. One day, we set out on a hike near Lake Superior, on the Lakeshore Trail in the Apostle Islands National Lakeshore. At the trailhead, we see a worm infestation in the surrounding forest. We decide to give the path a try anyway. All too soon we're brushing into the strings and collecting hitchhikers from the branches and brush. After a hundred yards, we're forced to retreat. When we reach the open parking area again, we pluck dozens of crawlers from each other's clothes. The silk will have to come off in the wash.

With the caterpillar masses in plain sight, predators could be expected. We've heard a few of our native birds go for them: nuthatches, chickadees, redwings, jays, and some warblers. I have yet to see this. They look tasty from a bird-food angle, but maybe they have a bad flavor.

After a week or so of worm encampment on our property, woolly white cocoons appear under the house eaves. They must be in the surrounding vegetation as well. I get out a broom and a ladder and knock them down off the buildings. They're well-fastened, stuck in place, requiring some real effort to bat loose. The crawlers themselves are almost gone. The shell-shocked trees, naked in mid-June, make a game effort and put out some meager greenery to get themselves some photosynthesized energy. We start to notice the "friendly flies," a parasitic species called *Sarcophaga aldrichi*. They're friendly because they tend to crawl on us; fortunately, they don't bite. They also carry out a friendly action, boring into the cocoons to deposit eggs. The fly larvae will hatch in a few days and start to make meals of the still-unhatched pupa. If not for these flies, there would be yet more worms in the outbreak. It's hard to imagine this could be; at their peak, worms are everywhere.

In a couple of weeks, when July arrives, so does the adult stage of the caterpillar. Tan, nondescript moths flap about our entryway light in bunches. They're out there having moth sex, something researchers tell us can last more than three hours, lucky devils. Then the eggs are deposited on the twigs of nearby trees and bushes. Oaks are favored, and we have many of them on the property. The nocturnal moths also have few predators and are able to get the task completed.

Fall comes, and I look out into the dusk. There are no worms, no moths. Only the eggs out there, waiting for spring and the next turn of the cycle. Was this the peak year, or will as many be back next summer, or will there be still more? There are outbreaks only when conditions are right, though what those conditions are is uncertain.

After a year or two, things taper off. The caterpillars become a rarity. We forget them. We'll know when they're returning only when we see the scouts of their creeping battalions start to march again.

Consuming

Almost everyone who lives in a house in the woods gets the lesson. Our first course came a few years earlier, while still living at the rental house a few miles away. One summer night I forgot to roll down the garage door. In the morning, I walked into the sunny summer yard and saw the yawning opening. Everything seemed unchanged, but then I realized my plastic trash can was gone. A trail of debris spread down the driveway. It was time to investigate, so I assembled my team. With six-year-old Eric and three-year-old Todd, I went off on the track of the garbage thief.

The can was in the ditch at the foot of the drive, undamaged except for a few scratch marks. Some of our trash was in the middle of the road. Picking up as we went along, we moved ahead through crushed grass and plants, into the dry marsh across the road. Fifty feet off the pavement, we found the place where the plastic bags had been ripped apart and the good stuff eaten. The bear was long gone, but we now knew that this was its neighborhood, where it was on patrol and checking in regularly for strong-smelling food left unattended in the night.

American Black Bear
Ursus americanus

At the new house a few years later, a thump against the big window at the foot of our bed woke me around two a.m. I rolled out and went to the deck light switch without grabbing my glasses. When I hit the lights, I could see black forms moving in the glare, one seemingly vaulting off the deck railing. Our theory is that the mother bear was standing outside the window in the flower garden, up on hind legs and batting at the hanging bird feeder, when she thumped the window. One or more of several cubs were on the adjacent deck railing, reaching for a second feeder that hung above. The cubs jumped off the deck when the lights came on, and everyone was gone into the black woods in a matter of seconds.

The feeders are now mostly hung from a strung wire between two skinny maples, as much to challenge the squirrels as to discourage the bears. We are more careful about times when bears are out, hanging feeders in fall when the snow has come, taking them down when warm, bear-waking days appear again, putting them out in the summer only when we're sure the bears have plenty of other feeding sources at hand.

On a canoe trip with a group of family and friends, we ventured into territory with a known problem bear. We were still casual about our food hanging methods, but this bear taught us a new attitude. It did quick work of taking down our limb hang and foraging through a food pack. We learned from others camped on the big lake that it ran a regular circuit of all the campsites, always visiting the tree in camp most favored for dangling a pack. In the next day we were able to move to an island campsite well offshore, where we shinnied up two small maples and hung our pack from a temporary lashed crosspole. Didn't matter; the bear swam out in the dark, found the hanging rig, and was crawling out on the crosspole to knock down the pack when my brothers chased it away. We've since learned the best way to avoid circuit-riding bears in camping areas is to seal the food up thoroughly, then put it in the brush well out of camp and off trail, in places where the bear doesn't go.

We walk through our woods and all of our northern country with full knowledge that one of our neighbors is bigger than us, with pointed teeth, long claws, and a taste for anything edible. Yet the bear is shy and has learned to move on when we come into view. For years I've looked into larger holes in the ground and under tangles of tipped-up tree roots, expecting some day to see a bear looking back, as my father once saw in the woods near our home. In my teen years, when the deer and bear hunting seasons ran at the same time, I once stood with rifle under my arm and watched a bear lope away from me up a slope. I let it go. My meeting with the bear could wait.

DARTING

Ruby-throated hummingbird
Archilochus colubris

What is it like to have instinct so deeply built into your brain that you have scarcely an original thought? You live a life of pure purpose and reaction. You are to feed, to mate, to find food for the nestlings. You are to fly unimaginable distances to avoid perishing from the cold. You are to protect your life from big, hungry attackers by dodging, by hiding. You are to move with speed and intent, to instantly act. What are "you," really, but a bundle of programmed chemicals, set loose for a brief existence?

Yet when I see the ruby-throat finish feeding at one of the flowers that ring the house, then curve away into the canopy on a path like a kite string, I feel a wave of joy in the tiny bird, a surge of power to go anywhere in our space. It's a peel-out, a rise into the unseen world that is there in the tall popples, oaks, and maples above us, places so near and yet so remote to us. Perched on a limb some place up there, the tiny cup of grass and twigs holds the fingernail-sized offspring, the center of the hummingbird's world.

We hung the feeder from the cedar-wood eaves of the house, close by our bedroom window and beside the deck. Water was boiled in the microwave, then infused with sugar and poured into the bottle-like reservoir. Change it regularly, so mold doesn't grow and sicken the birds. It's a lot of work, but not so much as keeping tiny beaks filled.

On a family vacation, we camped in the high desert of Dinosaur National Monument in Utah. In a small clump of arching cottonwoods, the campground hosts had set their trailer and put out a number of feeders. Whenever a feeder was refilled, a swarm of eager birds would instantly descend and buzz about the trailer, probing and pushing to get at the snack. The hosts would emerge from this hummingbird cloud, grinning in their task of entertaining both birds and campers.

Our feeder patrons don't make a swarm, but they come regularly and often. They too can be aggressive, chasing each other away. Once or twice, we've seen hummingbird-bee interactions, when large bees found some excess sweetness on the outside of the feeder. Hummingbirds will take small insects, but a bee is a little large for them; still, they could and did try to drive them off, chasing the circling bee in a kind of aerial ballet.

After the bears knocked down our first feeder, we went looking for a new one and found a feeder with perches at the base. What is this, we wondered. The hummingbird hovers to drink at flowers, and it certainly must prefer to hover at the feeder. But we gave it a try, and sure enough, the birds settled quickly onto the plastic twigs and stayed there, visibly gulping the sweet liquid. As they fed, we could look closely to admire their shiny olive-green backs and wing feathers, the deep sequin-y red of the bibs on the males, the incredibly small and strong toes and claws.

The young, yet smaller, must go through some fledgling flights somewhere up above us. They are never seen or heard; only the adults appear, yet their every action tells us nesting is happening. Perhaps with great patience and unlimited time, one could sit on the deck with binoculars, peering among the leaves, and find the tiny hummingbirds beginning to hover and zoom up there, smaller than the damselflies.

Lacking that patience, we're content to watch the quick movements of the birds at our large flowers. The stargazer lilies are favorites when they open, catching rainwater and sweetening it to draw in the bugs. The birds are also attracted, coming and going in an instant, bright green against the deep red and rose.

They leave early. By mid-July, the receding daylight must trigger something in that batch of programming. Little by little, the feeder visits dwindle away. When September is on the horizon, the feeder hangs near-full for days. By the middle of the month, it stays untouched. And then we know they are gone, taking the summer with them.

Perplexing

Mystery Bush
Species unknown

The bush stands among the maples and oaks, a few feet west of the driveway. It's just under knee-high, its crown about the size of a soccer ball. It lives most of the summer surrounded and shaded by the bracken and hazel. But in midspring, when the ferns are just fiddleheads, this woody little plant stands in plain view. And at this time, with its leaves still small and pale green, it bursts out in pairs of small, bell-shaped flowers of sun-bright yellow.

Our Audubon guide to the flowering plants of North America is a great tool, but in this case, it's not been much help. It couldn't be a twinflower, the most prominent producer of blossoms in twos; those grow as low, trailing plants with soft stalks and stems while this is solid and grayish in its stems and twigs. The yellow color of the blooms put other candidates off the list.

To remain an unknown is not a bad thing. Intrigue in a minor way provides a starting point for pleasant mental inquiry, for pondering why something is obviously so, yet doesn't fit the patterns. One could consider whether this bush was an exotic from the days when this was a farm, something planted for the dooryard. Or it could have taken a long ride as a seed, lofted along stuck to the foot of a migrating duck or in the gut of a nuthatch, then dropped here to take hold, against strong odds, and grow into a colorful puzzle.

Most appealing was the thought this might be something new. Could it be unique, not just to our yard, but to the planet? Some subtle shift in the genome could have changed the flower from another tone to the eye-catching yellow, for instance. We might be the owners of something never seen here before.

Our Western culture likes to put things into their proper boxes, with name labels attached so we can easily talk about them in a shared understanding. It's a handy reference system, though it comes with obvious limits. To call something by its species or common name, following the model set by Linnaeus, is to stereotype it. You may have seen one of these, but the next one might be something with a different look, a different feel. To more fully know my mystery bush, you should see it where it is, in the dry woods surrounded by gray tree-trunks and with ferns sprouting around it, making a bold statement about the warming of the earth at its roots. It seems to thrive here in its uniqueness. As it puts out flowers, it plays its role in the progress of all growing things. It works to give its putative children a chance to exist, to grow as it does. It says, "If I'm good, the world will have more of me."

"Good" is, of course, a very subjective quality. Down the hill and across the bay, purple loosestrife is "good" in the wetlands of the big lake, crowding out the native cattails that don't quite share its level of ambition. It was brought here because its decorative qualities were found good by people who wanted it for their gardens. But it was too good for its own good, and after moving into the wild, it is now too good for native plants we want to keep. The tale repeats, from the starling to the house sparrow, from the zebra mussel to the rusty crayfish, from the western cheatgrass to the Japanese knotweed that appeared uninvited in a ditch near our neighborhood, a gangling outbreak of heavy waving stalks and broad flapping leaves.

This little bush, though, doesn't seem to be here to crowd anything out, or to modify its place to suit its continued existence. It does good: it grows and flowers, it makes it through our testing winters, it continues to evoke thought. Its bold flowering means better days are ahead for us.

After years of dwelling on it, I cautiously conclude that it must be a form of *Diervilla*, the bush honeysuckle, even though the leaves aren't the right shape. Its reason for being here, far from others of its kind, continues to be a mystery.

DIVING

Great Northern Loon
Gavia immer

The sounds of our place in the world surround us. The most common are human sounds: cars on our road or on the county highway a few miles off, airplanes traveling from Duluth to Chicago a few miles up. You might think of people-made sounds as invasions of our quiet place, but some of them bring pleasant memories. We're surrounded on three sides by the larger lake. On warm summer afternoons, the buzz of outboard motors over the hill is the classic sound of northern resort country, evoking images of big wooden fishing plugs and grinning northern pike at the end of an arching rod. In the evening, I sometimes hear freight trains five miles away, about the distance this same line of tracks runs from my parents' home, many miles to the southeast. In my teenage years I would stand outside on subzero nights, looking at the stars and listening to the diesel engines whistle and pull through the Lemington crossing. Now that same sound is here in my adult life, comforting me with the knowledge that not everything has changed.

The sounds of the loons also come from a distance. Our lake is too small for them. Loons need plenty of aquatic tarmac to get up and going. While their performance in the water is exceptional, and their flight skills good enough for trips of great length and speed, the takeoff ability needs to evolve a few more millennia. Or maybe this is just one of evolution's compromises; the narrower wing size required for a slim, slippery diving bird may be optimized for just enough square inches of feathered lift to get off the water safely in the places they live. In any case, the place they love, with plenty of runway, is a somewhat larger, oblong lake just over the low ridge to the south. This entire lake is privately owned, with protected wild shoreline good for their nesting practice that puts them just inches from the water. From there we hear their hoots and wails when warm weather comes and know the creature that holds the heart of the North is back with us.

Just once have we seen a loon on our lake. On a fall day a wail came from nearby, and we walked down to the shore to see what was up. A mature adult was cruising out in the center, making smooth dives for the abundant panfish hiding under the lily pads that year. Maybe this loon just couldn't resist a private fishing hole, perfect for bulking up a bit before getting on the road to South Carolina or Louisiana.

The big bird stayed for several days. Its spooky calls came out of the dusk, reminding us all of its presence, Eric listening wide-eyed and whispering, "It's the loon." I began to wonder if it was having trouble getting off of the lake. The folks at the Sigurd Olson Environmental Institute in nearby Ashland have tales of rescuing loons who stayed too long, until the ice closed in and they were left paddling anxiously in a small open hole. Like us, wildlife have plenty of chances to make bad decisions.

A morning came when the lake was quiet, the sky gray as dusk. The bare maples and oaks arched over the shore, waiting for the ice crystals to creep out from the edge. I would like to have seen the loon go. It must have circled around and around the open water, calling out its tremolo flight song, corkscrewing up into the gray sky before pointing its bill toward warmer latitudes.

SLIDING

North American River Otter
Lontra canidensis

One of those gray afternoons of March, the time when it's too damp and melting to snowshoe or ski, too chilly to hike. The clinging winter hangs over everyone's emotions. It's hard to believe in blue skies or sunshine.

Eric, on the edge of teenage, looks up from his book and out the big living room windows. "Dad, what is that?"

Out on the lake ice, something is moving. Two black spots are wriggling away out there. Deb joins us with Todd, about to be a middle schooler. We watch the white surface and see an unexpected show.

Two otters are out there, doing what we've heard otters do. The snow on the surface is crusty. They run, a kind of humping gallop, then flop down and slide for yards. They play a kind of tag, edging each other across our view. It's a joyful chase across and around the frozen surface. The otters go again and again, full of energy, oblivious to the dreary surroundings.

"Where did they come from?" It's hard to give a definite answer. They must have been somewhere with a little open water, where they could get into a bank den under the ice. The best guess is from the lake just out of sight to the south; its shallow pans would be excellent otter habitat. But why would they trek more than a quarter mile, over a rise, to put on a sliding exhibition on our lake? Maybe otters also crave a change of scene at the end of a long winter, no matter how slight the difference in the view. They are intelligent, curious creatures. I think of paddling the chain of lakes at the head of the Manitowish River, where very early one morning we met three otters swimming upstream in a line. They popped heads up in comic sequence to peer at our canoe. They almost seemed to look right into our watercraft, perhaps to see if we might be throwback voyageurs hauling packs of the skins of their cousins. All we had were packs of damp tent and gear after a rainy night, so we passed them by on the starboard, admiring their smooth glide as they cruised onward.

Dusk came out on the ice before the otters ended their game. We saw them again a few months later, as we paddled around the lake in the open water of June. They were diving and rising as spirits of the water. We hoped then they had moved their base of operations to our shores, maybe tunneling a den into the soft matter and roots of the bog. But we did not see them again. Most likely the fishing, decimated by freeze-out, was not what they needed to survive here. They must have humped their way over the low ridge and back down into larger, more hospitable waters.

From our brief sightings, Todd grew a special love for the

otter. At the Great Lakes Aquarium in Duluth, he stood by the glass as captive otters slid down water-slicked stones. A stuffed-animal otter was added to the collections in his room. All of us kept one eye to the lake, hoping once again we would see the lively, joyful action of these animals living with the spirit to do something on a dull afternoon, just for the fun of it.

ANNOYING

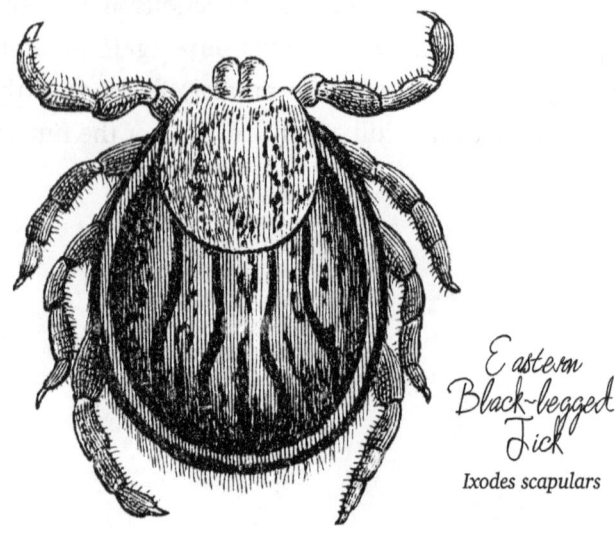

Eastern Black-legged Tick
Ixodes scapulars

When I was growing up in the northern Wisconsin woods, there were deer ticks, but they were a great rarity. Wood ticks were common. Every summer, your dog's ears would collect these bloodsuckers, and, if not yanked out, the gross arachnids would turn into bulging gray grapes. When you walked through the weeds or brush, in a matter of time you felt them creeping up your legs under your jeans. If you pulled up the fabric, they would inexplicably cling to it in some fashion, hiding from you until you dropped the pants back into place. It was as if they had evolved some superbug capability to leap outward the instant they sensed motion and snag onto the rough cloth. Soon, there was that crawly feeling again. Press down hard on the outside, feel the bugger squirming underneath, roll up the cloth until you can nab it. The ones you missed would make their furtive way to your hairline at the back of the neck, to your armpits, to the backs of your knees, or, in true nasty intent, to your groin. Then they'd latch on, and you'd find them, usually because of a persistent itch that suddenly made sense. They'd get away with some of your lifeblood, the nourishment they seek to fuel their egg laying. You'd flush them down the toilet with a vengeance. But these were not deer ticks.

Tiny as it was, the deer tick was also usually detected when scraping at an itchy spot. But you'd have to look twice. Yes, that speck has legs. Get a tweezers, grasp the hindquarters firmly, give a pull, and hope it comes away with a chunk of you in its mandibles. The alternative, where the head breaks off and is left gripping the flesh, is to always be avoided, since the bacteria and viruses that swim around in the tick's spit can continue to flow into you for some time.

Deer ticks were a rarity, and Lyme disease was undiscovered. It was not until the end of the 1970s you heard of it. There's a sickness you can get from those teeny ticks, we heard. Catch it early, and you could be all right, especially if you got some antibiotics. Catch it late, especially after the red ring forms and then fades around the bite— if it appears at all, sometimes it doesn't— and you just might be in for flu-like body aches, sore joints, or even a long-term litany of chronic symptoms that, to say the least, will spoil your lifestyle.

We watched the maps as more and more infected deer ticks were found in our territory. And we seemed to meet up with more and more of them. We started pulling up our socks over our pant legs when we went in the woods, wearing long sleeves even in the warmer summer months. We checked our hides when in the shower. But we knew the deer ticks were creeping about.

They struck Todd first. He earned his deer tick badge while at Scout camp near Rice Lake, seventy miles off to the south. After camp week was done, he went off to visit grandparents for a few days. When he came home, he showed us the red ring near his neck. A regimen of antibiotics followed.

A year or two later, I was putting a new coat of gray stain on the house siding. The next day I suddenly became aware of irritation under my watch band. I whipped the timepiece off. At first, I could barely see the black speck. Then, squinting more closely, I could make out the legs. It came off with tweezers and went with me in a bottle to the clinic, where I found the medical staff very uninterested in looking at yet another deer tick. In a day or two, my wrist was swollen and aching while I went through my supply of doxycycline tablets.

Both Todd and I dodged long-term effects of the disease. Todd had a few joint pains for a while that may have been Lyme or may have been a growth spurt. Thankfully, neither of us has had the debilitating effects that mess up the lives of others. Since my first incident, I've had half a dozen deer ticks, mostly collected in the course of my volunteer work for hiking trail maintenance along the North Country Trail. I find them, usually by itch, I get them off, and I get the antibiotics. But I keep hearing how antibiotics should be used only when necessary. So I think about more ways to avoid picking up this persistent pest.

The real problem is the *Borellia* virus—either *burgdorferi* or *mayonii*—that grows in the tick's saliva glands in warm weather, spending the cold months in the gut of some vertebrate. Deer or deer mice are the favorites, but birds can also carry the tick and fly it away into new ranges.

When I was growing up, I read books about the scourges

of more distant, warmer places. Malaria was the bane of the tropics, killing more people than any other sickness. A friend's father had contracted it in the Philippines during the war and sometimes still broke out in shivers. Maladies like dengue fever were out there, too. Somewhere in the West there was Rocky Mountain spotted fever, carried by some sort of exotic tick unlike our common ones. But illness inflicted by bugs wasn't part of our lives.

I wondered at the time if this would ever change. Would some mutation of malaria suddenly infest our ever-present mosquitos? That was the thing I almost expected. I didn't think at all about the minuscule ticks. But the tick has now answered my question, and with the climate changing, the prospect of mosquito-borne disease is hardly off the table. West Nile virus is in the area, and La Crosse encephalitis creeps northward. I walk down by the lake and listen to the steady drone on an early June evening while swatting at the vampires zipping in to puncture my epidermis. It seems only a matter of time.

Glowing

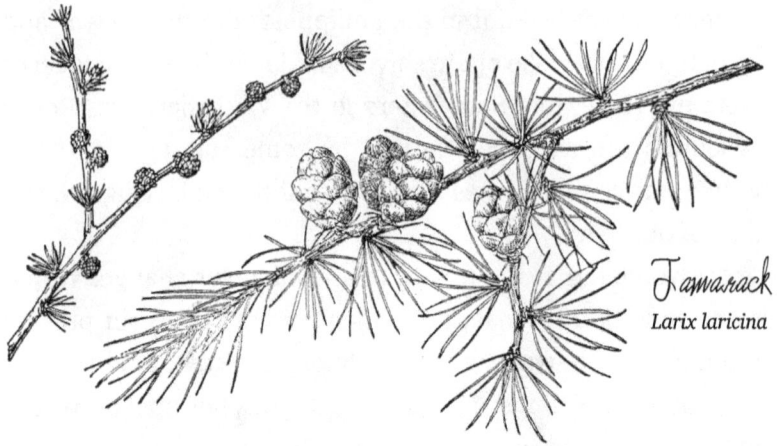

Tamarack
Larix laricina

We've seen the lake in both low and high water. A few years ago, we entered a drought cycle. As the water sank, I noticed a rounded white shape just under the surface, not far from the narrow vee in the shoreline where we slide the canoe in. Instantly I thought of a skull. It could be someone ancient, from prehistory. Then too, it just might be the victim of a more recent murder, one of those people who vanish and just never turn up. Just our luck to have something like this appear on our land. But I couldn't see it closely and chose not to probe at it. In the next year the water sank a few inches more. I was relieved to now find my imagined skull with gaping eyeholes was simply a glacier-rounded lump of whitish granite, its sockets just cavities from gas bubbles. It was something much, much older than any human skull, probably older than any bones, human or otherwise. It was a remainder from volcanic eras when life, if it existed, was soft-bodied.

In a couple more years, the "skull rock" had emerged and now lay on the new shoreline, surrounded by mud and ever-ambitious grasses. Not far away, something unexpected came up. In the spring it was chartreuse green, bristling with fine needles. In the late fall, it turned gold, then shed its needles to stand bare and skeletal. It was a tamarack, the most distinct of our conifers. It might have seeded from the lone small tamarack in the heart of the nearby bog. Or it could have been from a seed brought by a bird from westward, over the hill and across the narrow arm of the big neighbor lake, where acres of tamarack grow in a swamp at the marshy creek mouth.

Tamarack, spruce, and willow are the trees of the boreal forest, the sub-arctic region that begins at the north shore of Lake Superior. A few boreal patches lie on the Wisconsin south shore, and from these, tamarack extends out across nearly all of our state. Minnesota has tamarack forests that blaze golden in the fall, before the needles drop off. It grows there in all parts that aren't prairie. It's found in all of Michigan, mostly in mixed forests. It's in New England and New York. But this is the south of its range. It's really a tree of Canada, of the taiga that runs up to the arctic tree line.

A few years pass and the tamarack has grown to my mid-thigh. Now, though, the rains and snows have come back. The little tree stands through the summer with its feet in the water, surrounded by the edge species such as wild iris and reeds. It won't mind this; soggy spots are really its favorite habitat. What's more unusual is to find a tamarack growing up on a hillside or a ridgeline. Yet it can live and thrive there, too.

The Anishinaabe found tamarack good for making snowshoes; that's what the original version of its name means. The inner bark has medicinal uses. But it's small for lumber and grows where harvesting isn't easy, so it's mostly left alone. It may be best loved by the white-throated sparrow, the bird that sings "Oh sweet Canada, Canada, Canada" from the cool, shady heart of tamarack bogs.

As I pull the canoe up on the shore and turn it over under the big oak, I take note of the water level over the top of the skull rock. It's just an inch or so now. But it seems likely it will vanish once again as the lake deepens. Then it will just be my story, unless someone else spots it again and, like me, mistakes its odd shape for something sinister.

Pursuing

Fisher
Pekania pennanti

She came from the farm, from the place in west central Wisconsin where Deb grew up, among fields, among woodlands of big oaks and maples. There were two mewing kittens in a box, with Eric and Todd peering in, trying to choose. It was hard to pass up the calico, so she rode home with us in a newly purchased cat carrier. She cried out part of the way, while the two boys talked quietly to her to give comfort.

The idea was that she would live in the attached garage for a while. That lasted less than a day. She moved in, made herself comfortable in a spot on the rocking chair where the midday sun warmed the cushion. In time, we joked that she owned the house. She rested where she pleased, ate when there was food, and became our quiet, attentive companion.

She was named Rice, by Eric, in some connection with a Scout camp friend who came from Rice Lake. Rice had white fur, to be sure, on her belly and the backs of her legs, on her chin, and in splotches on her front legs and paws. But most of her coloration was a deep gray mottled with patches of dark brown. Here and there were clumps of almost-black, and on one leg a bit of near-orange. The whole effect was handsome, as if she had been painted by an impressionist. Georges Seurat could have placed her on his afternoon lawn, where she would have graced the scenery and activity.

Life with us was placid for Rice. She was allowed to roam about the outdoors part of the time; generally she stayed in the yard or prowled the woods between the house and lake. Soon she was back at the door, calling to come in. When not on the sun-heated rocker, she would snuggle up on one of the boys' bedcovers, napping away the day as only a well-fed house cat can. When we came home from work and school, she often greeted us at the door, ready for a little attention and dinner.

A day of excitement for Rice came in her first year. On a late summer afternoon, she was outdoors with the kids when a golden retriever dashed into the yard. It spotted a quarry and ran Rice around the front of the house. When we caught up with this classic dog-cat race, the marauding dog was leaping about in the woods, the cat nowhere to be seen. "Dad, look up!" the boys called. I did, but saw nothing. "Look higher!" Rice was hunched on the top of a dead oak snag, fully twenty feet up. Her nervously shifting paws showed a lack of confidence in her perch. She had got there on pure adrenaline and feline instinct and only now had a moment to think about where she was or what might happen next.

I chased off the lolloping dog, never to be seen again. Back in the woods, a cat rescue was launched, involving a ladder, a long pole, a basket, cat treats, and pleading calls to Rice, exhorting her to move to this makeshift elevator. She wasn't having it. A tentative foray with a front paw was made, but she would go no farther. The snag was straight, and the top looked incredibly high; how would she come down without breaking her neck?

Two hours of futile effort went by. Then it began to get dark. Since Rice wouldn't come down, she would stay where she was. There were expressions of worry, of fear. But then, just as the dusk was getting too dense to see much, there was a scrabbling above and a thump at the foot of the tree. In the way of most cats, Rice had got herself down. She made a streak for the house door, where she was caught up and closely examined. No damage was found, and Rice came in to an ample dinner in celebration of her self-rescue from both dog and tree.

A few years later, Eric was asked to care for a neighbor's cat at their home for a few days while the owners were away. This aging cat had diabetes and required a daily insulin shot. Eric learned how to calm the cat, grab its loose neck fur, and inject the drug.

Not more than a year later, after Rice passed her ninth birthday, Deb noticed that Rice was having urinary problems. A visit to the vet confirmed that she, too, had feline diabetes. She would require insulin twice a day, morning and evening. Eric taught each of us the technique. She would never enjoy it, but the shots extended her days with us.

As fall approached that year, Rice simultaneously became more restful and more restless. She would nap longer, then go outside and venture off, out of sight. Her absences became longer. Then came a day when, after going out for her morning walk, Rice didn't return when called. We had to leave for work and school. But in the late afternoon, we came home to find her sitting by the deck door, patiently expecting us.

A week later, she went out in the morning and sat on the doormat, wind ruffling her fur, looking out toward the lake. I watched her, knowing she might take off for the day again. I turned away; when I looked back, she was gone, off the deck and out of my sight. Sure enough, she didn't return when called.

That evening we had a high school football game to attend. Eric had moved on to college while Todd was in the high school pep band. Our schedule was tight. We might have been able to go home to let Rice in, but there wasn't much time. I decided we would go directly to the game and home afterward. Todd was distraught with worry about Rice, and I wondered if I'd made the best decision.

Rice wasn't waiting for us when we came home. In the days that followed, I walked the woods throughout the neighborhood, calling for her, looking for a sign. There was none.

The neighbors said, "You know there's a fisher around." These large weasels are predators of the porcupine, but a house cat is an easier and somewhat less prickly catch.

Rice was older and less well, less able to run and climb. And a tree would be no sanctuary from a fisher, which lives among the branches as often as not.

We never saw the fisher, but two other cats down the road disappeared, so it was there, doing what it does. I don't begrudge it taking the life of our wandering pet, though I will always regret not going back that evening before the game. We were lucky to have Rice while she was with us, and I think of her curled on my lap, purring as I stroke her beautiful coat. She will always be part of our story, part of our family.

Persisting

Northern Paper Wasp
Polistes fuscatus

The neighborhood always has its paper wasp nest in the warm months. One of the minor skills of getting by in this place in the forest is keeping track of where the nest is. The wasps love shelter, so under the eaves of a tool shed or in the peak of a house gable is prime real estate. Spot the nest in the early stage, just baseball-sized or smaller, and you can deter later difficulties. After the removal, the wasps relocate, usually to a tree limb. One year it was on the northeast side of the yard, far from the house, though close to the shed where mower and snowblower spend their down time. I kept an eye on it when rattling the mower out of its lair or running it past the tree where the nest was lurking. Another year, it was hung from a limb high over the blacktop road, a dangling lantern ornament among the leaves as you drove or hiked below. Some years it would be discovered only at end of season, when exposed by the dropping leaves. Oh, so *that's* where they built it this time around.

You may also find the nest where you don't expect it. One warm July day, I tipped up a ladder to do some rain gutter fix-it work on the shaded north side. Wham! Two stings in rapid fire. I skidded down fast, made a short sprint to a safe distance, and checked out my new welts. The nest was not more than three feet from the ladder, tucked under the soffit and hard to see. It was grapefruit-sized and surrounded by annoyed, swirling insects.

In the old house where I grew up, alongside the Couderay River, wasps were occasional summer visitors. We would knock the nascent nests off the house, but the nearby trees provided many choices for relocation. A roving insect would unexpectedly appear, hovering in the dining area or the family room. My father was allergic to most kinds of stings. The appearance of the threatening hymenopter called for an all-out assault with tools at hand: flyswatters, rolled newspapers, books, paper towels. I grew up learning to mistrust the ornery bugs, and periodic stings in the wild reinforced my attitude. I didn't inherit my father's allergy, but I also know such sensitivities can come over time; in fact, his allergy developed this way. So I'm always careful around stinging insects and pay close attention to my vitals when stung.

In adulthood I've learned wasps, like everything else, have their place in the ecology. Like their distant relatives, the honeybees, they spread some pollen around. Wasps often eat troublesome insects, especially larvae. They sometimes serve, nest and all, as lunch for bears and other climbing critters that don't mind stings. But relations between wasps and humans have their limits. They are fiercely protective of their home and tend to swarm about in ways that just make us uncomfortable. Better they build their gray lanterns out in the woods, the place where they're adapted to survive, a place away from people disruptions.

One of our traditions is to go each autumn to the hills above Bayfield. Out in the county forest, in a place my parents came upon long ago, we pick wild apples from an abandoned orchard. It's back on a rough track traveled by log trucks and bear-dog haulers, full of potholes and twisty with clay. We once again drink deeply the autumn-painted views across a deep valley, up to the pine-trimmed ridge top. On this long-lost homestead we hunt firm, solid fruit on the branch, usually green or striped in red, very good for pie, sauce, and cider. We also know the swollen, yellow apples with red streaks are full of sweetness, tend to go to mush, and are early on the ground. Wasps crawl there, hover, and nibble at the fruit. We move cautiously among the windfalls, grabbing a few of these sugar bombs off the tree, placing them gently into the old slatted bushel.

In this place, I spent the first moments with my partner-to-be, the young woman invited along by friends to meet a person of many enthusiasms, some very much over-the-top. As I clambered up into the branches of the bent, weathered tree, reaching for the handsome apples just beyond my grasp, she stood below and stepped carefully around the insect-laden windfalls, catching the harvest I passed down to her. So have we moved forward through so much living, both stung at times, but with a kind of care and humility to pass among nature gently, enjoy its fruits, and respect the ways of those living alongside us.

STRIKING

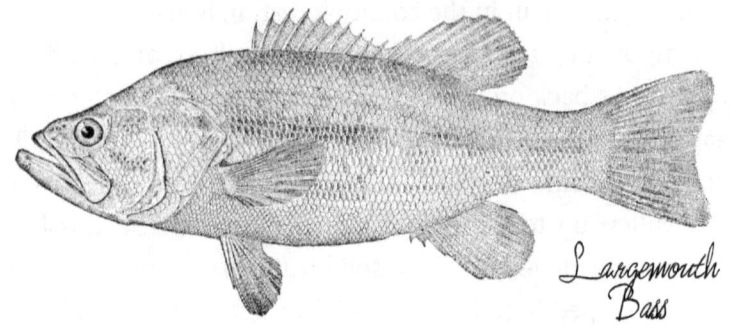

Micropterus salmoides

Some years, there are fish. Other years, there aren't. Not a puzzlement, just a fact of nature.

With five-year-old Eric, I carry the blue and white canoe from the road down to the shore. There's no house and no path yet; those are still more than a year away. Thick ferns, hazel brush, and blackberry canes grab at the legs of my jeans as we push our way toward water. It's early summer, cool and sunny. We're out to find out if there's fishing at our future home.

Life jackets and paddles in place, rods ready and hooks baited, we push off among the lilies. I have Eric set up with the traditional rig: bobber, sinker, hook and worm. I'm casting a Twister bait, dropping it right at the edge of the lily pad mats.

The lake is calm, the sky blue with a few high clouds to take off the glare. A couple of mallards are working the shoreline weeds for the succulent water plants they love. Crows call from back in the high pines, and there are songbirds flitting branch-to-branch along the shore. It couldn't be nicer.

It's not long before Eric has a fight on. He sets his lip firmly and cranks as the fish tugs. It pops flapping out of the lake, a bluegill about the size of his hand. I'm still on fishhook duty, so I grab the panfish, carefully avoiding the prickly dorsal, work the hook out of its mouth, display it for Eric to remember, then drop it back into its green, weedy world.

In an hour we catch a dozen or more, all 'gills. Most are twins of the first catch. Eric suspects we caught the same fish five times. My thought is we have a lake full of stunted bluegills, an overpopulation that holds all to about the same size. We keep a few, slightly larger ones to take home for dinner, mostly to show Deb and two-year-old Todd what the fish in our future lake are like.

Nearly two years later, we are looking toward the lake from our new home as the spring thaw sets in. We arrived in September and were preoccupied all fall in making the place comfortable and reasonably organized. The canoe is down on the shore, but we didn't get to dip a paddle before freeze-up. We watched winter creep in by mid-November and the lake become ice locked. Now the white cover is pulling back from the shoreline, exposing a narrow band of black water.

That's not what's catching our attention. We're looking at a flock of ring-billed gulls that has set up camp on the ice. They stand on the frozen surface making a racket; they squawk, flap, and dive. Deb asks, "Is this normal?" I shrug; I'm new here, after all. Maybe this is just a favorite migration stop for this noisy bird band.

The seagull show goes on for a couple of days. Eventually the ice is gone, warm weather returns, and we push the canoe out once more into bright open water. Eric and I fish an hour again, but results are completely different from the last expedition's. No bites, no tugs, no swirls, no fish. We work the shores and the pads, but nobody's home. It could be a bad day for the bite, but other days produce no results.

Our lake has frozen out. The correct term is winterkill, but neither of these terms really explains the natural disaster that has quietly passed in front of our windows. Heavy snow cover on the ice filtered out the sunlight passing to the water plants below. The plants turned down their oxygen output; dying plants joined the general muckiness on the lake bottom in soaking up dissolved oxygen instead. In this reversal of fortune in the oxygen budget, the fish were the losers.

Now we understand the gull ice party. It was a dead-fish orgy. We remember, too, a few swooping eagles getting in on the big feed. Somehow we hadn't noticed the fish corpses in the water.

Our neighbors let us know it had all happened before. "The fish should come back. It'll take a while." Somewhere under the ice, a few tough customers survived, or maybe eggs waited to hatch down on the bottom. They would eventually repopulate our aquatic desert.

Two years pass. Another spring day. Just checking, I toss the Twister bait out of the canoe toward the pads. Something grabs it, and I pull in the newcomer. It emerges, not blue-green and fin-flapping, but trim and tiny, yellow-white with orange fins. It's a small yellow perch. This species is a known winterkill survivor. We haven't met here before, but further fishing confirms it and its siblings are thriving in the lake.

On my next outing, my bait attracts something altogether different. It dashes for the weeds, tugs and battles, rushes back toward the canoe, then bursts from the surface: a largemouth bass. About ten inches long, in fact. As I admire its deep green back and sides before returning it to the lake, I think about how four-inch perch are likely to be the favorite chow on its personal menu. I catch more of those as well, but continue to find fighting bass, all of a size, commanding the shaded waters between weeds and lake bottom.

For the next few years, we are entertained by our growing bass population. Todd chortles as a green-and-white dancer, fourteen inches or so, skips across the surface in a series of bends and twists. My friend Ray comes to visit, and we spend a memorable couple of hours working around the shore, every second cast grabbing the attention of a bullying bass. Perch and the very occasional bluegill are also reeled in, but what we now live on is a bass honey hole.

The southwest corner of the lake, swampy with drowned logs, is superb fish structure. Todd and I paddle up one day to tease out the bass. He pitches his Rapala far back over the sunken stuff. There is an explosive splash, and his rod is bent double. Quicker than thought, there is a sound like a pistol shot. The broken monofilament rockets back toward his quivering hands. The look we exchange says it all: "WHAT-WAS-THAT?" It was the biggest predator in the lake, the Basszilla, is what. When we share the story with our fish-hunting neighbor, he nods knowingly. "There's a big one back there, all right. Maybe twenty-three inches." I think of the "hawgs" hunted in steamy southern reservoirs, a type of underwater goliath with a scoop so big it can engulf puny panfish without even tasting.

It's been more than ten years since the freezeout. Spring moves in again. Then the eagles begin to swoop. No gulls appear, but we look in the narrow band of chilly water between icecap and shoreline, and this time we see the panfish scattered on the bottom, victims of an event they could not begin to comprehend, trapped in theirlandlocked world. Yeah, we had a good run of it. Maybe the bass will come back.

The next few years are ones of uncertainty. I don't have much time to try fishing, and when I do, I catch nothing, except the sense of peace that comes with time spent quietly drifting on the water, watching the clouds pass. The fish just don't seem to be making their magic reappearance this time. Or maybe we had several freezeouts in a row. Then comes a spring day...the canoe again, the weeds again, the Twister bait. The sun is on me, and it could be a time machine, sending me back nearly two decades, in my blue canoe like Elton John singing "Where to Now, St. Peter?" Under the lilies, something seizes the bait, fights the line, and I pull out...a ten-inch crappie. The beefy, dark-green, speckled master of panfishes curls in my hand, longing with fishy energy for the freedom it will soon regain.

"Hello," I tell the crappie. "Where'd you come from?"

Wandering

White-Tailed Deer
Odocoileus virginianus

The deer drift through like ghosts, moving silently on paths of their own, often seen and sometimes sensed. One might step out the front door, feel a presence, and, looking to the right, see the doe and her yearling standing a few yards away on the grass. They gaze intently, then move quickly together into the woods, tails raised to signal their anxiety.

They are here in early winter, leaving their tracks stitched across any new snowfall. Their dark fall coats blend in with the gray trunks of maple and oak. As the season passes on, they become scarce. It's said they go down by the Brule River, into the cedar thickets and swamps there, where the flat, green needles they love are abundant.

If the winter is not too hard on them, they come back in the spring bright and glossy, almost pumpkin orange in their summer coats. The does don't really show it, but most are expecting. When the second week of May shows up on the calendar, they're looking for sheltered places to give birth. Usually there are twins. We see them, shaky at first on their skinny props. Then a week or two later they are full of jump, bounding high and far when startled. They've been taught to lie still and not move a muscle. But if discovered by a bear or wolf, bound they must.

The summer woods are full of green browse, but, for reasons unknown to us, the non-native things we plant around the house are special deer delicacies. I grew a garden and soon learned a three-foot fence was not enough to keep out these leaping ungulates. I needed five-feet high of sturdy wire to discourage them. The decorative hosta plant, with its thick green leaves, is always a favorite. A droopy-eyed Todd announced on one warm morning, "I couldn't sleep. A deer was crunching outside my window all night." Deb's hostas were neatly cropped down to the ground. On other occasions, a flower planter and a juniper bush became deer midnight snacks. Various repellents were applied: mothballs, sprays, geraniums, marigolds. The deer have been sometimes discouraged but always come back for at least a nibble.

When this was the Pinery, moose and elk were the dominant hoofed animals living among the big trees. A few deer may have been in the openings of the nearby sand barrens, in the edge-of-forest habitat they prefer. The big clearcut of the early twentieth century knocked down the woods and opened the sky for new shoots to grow. Elk and moose went north while deer populations grew. The mid-twentieth century was the time of the big "Up North" hunts, the growing hunter population chasing quarry in the farthest reaches of the state, like our neighborhood. The forest returned, and deer numbers went back down. But any time there's logging, the deer make a small recovery there.

No animal stirs more controversy in our state than the whitetail, and nowhere is there more controversy than here in the North. Researchers and auto insurance agents agree we have more deer than our habitat can sustain, to the detriment of fenders and the forest understory. The hunters will always want more deer, other impacts be damned. As a hunter of many years, though few kills, I have taken my pleasure from being in the late fall woods, good weather or bad, the woods that belong to the deer.

Back in our little woods, the deer are not resident; they have a larger patch of forest and swamp right down the road to enjoy, and there they spend most of their lives. Yet on a bright morning, drinking my coffee at the dining table, I've watched a young doe get up from her bed under the white pine by the shore, step to the lake for a drink, then wander off upslope, grazing on the fresh new growth. I wondered if she had snacked on the hostas last night.

Uplifting

Paper Birch
Betula Papyrifera

When we came here, something had already happened to the birches. Their white boles were scattered through the woods between the house and the lake, some slim and curving with elegance, others bigger and stolid. But they were dead, nearly all of them. No one was quite sure why. It could have been an insect invasion that swept through a few years earlier. Or maybe the drought had killed them. We were in a dry period, one that would go on for years. Birch love to have their feet in damp places, which is why their lovely white trunks grace the shores of most of our lakes. Then again, birches are a short-lived tree. Surrounded and shaded by taller maples and oaks, their time may simply have passed.

Birch limbs and trunks were scattered in our woods, evidence the dead trees were coming down. Eric and I walked among them toward the lake. While visiting a friend, he had gotten involved in tree house construction, returning home filled with enthusiasm for getting up among the branches and enjoying the view. Now we were looking for the place to start his own project.

Popples and maples didn't have much to offer but straight, tall trunks. Our few pines were too bushy. Oaks had possibilities but weren't in the right places. Then we saw it: a clump of three birches, nicely placed near where the bog and the lake met. It was easy to picture a triangular platform about ten feet up, with a view of the lake and the house. This was the place.

Of course, the birches were dead. One had snapped off about twenty feet up. The other two trunks had shed branches, but all three were solid to the hammer. One could have a crow's nest here for a while.

We nailed 2x4s between the trunks, laid down decking, and put a sturdy railing in place. Then we cut and nailed up crosswise more 2x4s to serve as a ladder. That's all that was needed. Here was a place where you could stand and hear the wind in the nearby pine, look out across the water, and dream about the next adventure.

Not all the birches had been taken by their unknown affliction. A large one stood by the path, not far from the lake. It might have been big enough for the most famous use of the paper birch, as the raw material for canoes, the transportation tool invented and put to greatest use by the Algonquian nations—notably by the Anishinaabe who lived, and still live, right here. It could be peeled, stitched together with spruce roots, then sealed with pine tar to produce the large sheets of bark needed for watercraft. The truly large canoe birches are a rarity in our forests today, but in centuries past they were there when needed, the source for frail but serviceable boats to ride the northern lakes and rivers.

A live, slim young birch stands just off the deck. Somehow

it, too missed the plague or resisted the drought. Its fresh buds come early in the spring, its light green leaves brightening the deeper colors of summer. It has a bit of a curve to it, an artistry of shape, pleasing the eye. It stretches a handful of branches upward in optimism. It might have been shaded out, but the opening for the house will give it access to sunlight for many years. It may also grow to be a canoe birch, a broad pale trunk marked with black, defying its short-lived nature.

Down by the lake, the treehouse served its years. The supporting trunks became softer, moisture collecting inside the wrapping of bark, hastening decay. Pieces broke off in the wind and fell down on the decking. One fall day I took the wrecking bar and pulled the structure loose, removing it for safety. The kids weren't around to help. They were off to high school and college, finding the adventures they may have dreamed about up among the rustling branches.

SHELTERING

Eastern Phoebe
Sayornis phoebe

I wonder if the makers of home entryway lights know the importance of their products to the survival of a species of small, gray-brown, white-bellied, black-billed birds. Our flat-topped plastic fixture, sheltered by overhanging eaves, was not just something to illuminate the steps or welcome visitors. It was a phoebe magnet.

My brother Doug, visiting from his home in the foothills of Virginia, spotted the nest-decorated light. "I've got one of those lights too, and the bird comes every year." Across North America, thousands of front doors must open onto phoebe habitat.

The first sign came each spring with splatters of mud and sphagnum on the wall below the globe. As days passed, a structure emerged above, neatly fitted to the circular shape of the flat surface. In less than a week, there was a finished nest, with a phoebe seated determinedly on it. The flighty bird would flutter away quickly if we came out the door, usually settling on the maple just a few feet away, watching as it tipped its tail downward in the phoebe's signature motion. Not more than a minute later, it was back on the nest at work on its task, which was to daily produce a small pinkish egg. When there were five, the egg-laying was done. With Eric or Todd watching, I held a mirror above the nest when the parent-to-be was away so we could admire this work of nature at our front steps.

The adult bird always flew off in the daytime when we came by, but by night she stuck firmly on the nest. Stepping out only when necessary, we quickly glanced, eye-to-eye, at our neighbor. She would return a passive stare, without moving a feather, but no doubt pleased when we moved on into the dark.

In ten days or so, the mirror revealed five gray, fuzzy balls where the eggs had been. Twitching and gaping, the hatchlings lived for nourishment. The second parent phoebe now made an appearance, and both dominated the yard, putting on an aerial demonstration of their family title, "tyrant flycatcher." Swoops at flying bugs usually concluded with a landing at the nest and a quick deposit in one of the wide-open beaks. We were grateful for their service in the control of our hardy crop of flies and mosquitoes and entertained by their fervent action in support of the newborns.

Ten days, perhaps two weeks, and hatchlings were feathered out. They huddled in a clump, overflowing their sheltered home, wings drooping off the edge of the nest, five beady glares eyeing us. We knew then it would be a matter of just hours. At some point, all at once, the five young would explode into flight, diving across the yard and into the trees. Once or twice the departure happened when we opened the door, the entry suddenly filling with flapping tiny phoebes, just as quickly gone and almost vanished, just a glimpse or two up in the greenery. Most times they would just be gone when we looked, having chosen their own right moment to get on with their lives. Either way, they never returned to the nest; their decision was all-in. I would think of them exploring the world they'd only seen from the narrow view out our entryway, thriving on the power of instinct and thousands of years of genetic history. I knew the world was a tough place for any young thing, and that some of our phoebes would soon be food for bigger predator birds or other hungry varmints. Still, the idea that they were out there somewhere, getting their bearings and starting to bulk up for the coming fall migration—something that was engraved in their being, since they had no way of learning it—was an encouraging thought.

Two days, three at the most, and if it was no later than mid-June, the mother was back on the nest, laying her daily egg and starting the process all over again. The second family grew just as the first. When they left for the trees in early July, I wondered if they met any of their more experienced siblings out there, rambling through the sky by the lake's edge and mopping up the mosquitoes.

In the beginning, I took down the nest every fall. The splattering mud and moss in the spring eventually persuaded me to save work for both myself and the birds by leaving the nest; it was put right back to use in the next year. Not a perfect solution, though. After a couple of years, it began to look lopsided. When I pulled the hardened earth and dry vegetation off the fixture, I discovered a new nest had been stacked on top of the original.

Every year, the phoebe was there. Did the original bird return again in the spring? Songbirds live only a few years at most. Did her daughters, granddaughters, and great-granddaughters come back to nest where they had been born, the memory of our sheltered light now a matter of phoebe tradition? There was no way of knowing. I like to think this phoebe family knew there was a good place here, among the millions of places they might have flown to nest. Whatever birds they were, their calls of phoebe, phoebe echoed through our windows across the years, and stepping out the front entry usually brought a view of a small, lively bird, perched on a lower branch, tail feathers dipping, ready to launch whenever a wandering bug buzzed into range.

Twenty-three years, and the phoebe was always there. Then came a spring with a few dabs of sphagnum by the light, but nothing more. No nest built, no clutch of five eggs, no hungry hatchlings. We glimpsed a phoebe or two around the yard, heard their calls at a distance, but they weren't living with us. At the end of the season, raking leaves from the flower garden, I found a dead adult phoebe lying below one of the windows. It was the year we put the house up for sale.

IN THE END

The days passed, became years. There were early springs, late thaws. There were epic blizzards, ice storms, rain in torrents. There were days of summer when the ripples on the lake danced endlessly, swirled by a canoe paddle only to sparkle again. There were days of fall, fine days to take a walk down the road amid the spiral of leaves. There were days of deep winter when the maples cracked and the oaks creaked, days to strap on snowshoes and feel the bite of the season. There were nights: nights of pattering rain on the roof we owned, nights of wind and worry. There were nights of full moon and warm air, the frogs singing a mighty chorus in honor of the greatness of it all.

There were school plays in the old auditorium, teacher conferences in the musty, lively classrooms. Scout meetings, track meets, basketball games. There were changes at work to deal with, deadlines to meet, travel to meetings, worries about budgets, good news of promotions. There were visitors: leading cousins back through the bog on snowshoes, spruce and tamaracks topped with Seussian snowcaps, studying tiny tracks in the whiteness. Sitting with the grandparents in the crowd at the band concerts; sleeping a crowd of canoeists, dreaming of the road north toward Canada at dawn.

There were loves and losses, friends and good neighbors. There were expeditions: down the nearby Brule, away to the Boundary Waters, to Isle Royale, to the Chippewa Flowage, to the windy Lake Superior beaches. There was joy, and there was tragic news. Eventually there were plans: college plans, trips to campuses, packing and moving to dorm cubicles, the hallway at home now echoing with the new quiet. There were eventually plans for a new home in a place we loved, not far away, close to the power and wonder that is Lake Superior.

All of this happened in the flow of time.

Yesterday we signed the deed that conveyed our 0.69 acres to new owners. We spent years preparing for this day, then months packing and moving the large collection of the things that had gathered around our lives. We walked down the narrow, curving path to sit on the bench by the lake and feel its presence just one more time. The day was breezy, and the sun shone, like hundreds of days we had known in this place. Winter would be here soon, but this day could go on in our memories forever.

Now we are people who once owned a place on water. A younger family will learn to love the place that was ours. They'll meet the neighbors: those plants and creatures that surrounded our lives and colored our days, the human neighbors who were always there for us.

For me, there will always be a feeling of wonder as I think of it, wonder that it all really happened. So many memories are centered by this place, this home. It was hard to give it up. But I have learned another thing while living my life here. I've learned that home is wherever the people you love are.

The memories will start to fade. But perhaps once every few years we'll drive by, just to see the place that was our home. And to glimpse again, through the trees, the bright water beyond.

Acknowlegements

To Deb, who has lived with this project for more than ten years, thank you. With much love.

Thanks to designer and creative thinker par excellence, Jamey Penney-Ritter, for her dedication to this project.

The public domain graphics leading each essay are primarily from the Biodiversity Heritage Library, www.biodiversitylibrary.org. A secondary source is the 1903 book, *Following the Deer*, by William J. Long.

Dr. Deborah Davis Schlacks helped make this a better book. Much needed, and much appreciated.

My late cousin, Kathy Muggenburg Smith, encouraged my writing. I recommend her many books, published as by Kate Watterson, which continue in print.

My parents, Mary L. Nordgren and David E. Nordgren, gave their children the freedom of the forests, rivers, lakes and woods. This book is one small way I can repay the gift.

My teachers Dolores Dygart, Florence Pasanen, Eugene Koci, Paul Quail, Chester Fraley, Larry Abrams, and Lloyd Williams guided my learning of the world around me.

This book is also for Ida Nordgren and Aldo Nordgren. I hope they'll find this a guide to what mattered for the family that came before them.

Peter D. Nordgren grew up around Couderay in northwest Wisconsin, where his family's business was canoes. He graduated from Winter Schools and earned a B.S. from the University of Wisconsin-Superior, M.S. from the University of Wisconsin-Stout, and Ph.D from the University of Minnesota.

He is the founder of WXPR Public Radio in Rhinelander, and among the founders of WOJB at Lac Courte Oreilles, KMHA in northwest North Dakota, and KUWS in Duluth-Superior. He has taught and worked at Bemidji State University and Nicolet College, and is professor emeritus of library science at the University of Wisconsin-Superior.

Paddling, XC skiing, and hiking while maintaining the North Country National Scenic Trail are among his and Deb's retirement activities. He occasionally writes for *Silent Sports* magazine.

www.ingramcontent.com/pod-product-compliance
Lightning Source LLC
Chambersburg PA
CBHW020459030426
42337CB00011B/163